THE COMPLETE GUIDE TO

Blacksmithing

Horseshoeing, Carriage and Wagon Building and Painting

Based on the

Text Book on Horseshoeing

By

Professor A. Lungwitz

With Chapters on

Carriage-Ironing, Wagon and Buggy Painting, Varnishing, Ornamenting, Etc.

By

Charles F. Adams

With a New Foreword
By
Dona Z. Meilach

ILLUSTRATED

BONANZA BOOKS
NEW YORK

Copyright © 1981 by Crown Publishers, Inc.
All rights reserved.

This edition is published by Bonanza Books,
a division of Crown Publishers, Inc.

h g f e d c b a

BONANZA 1981 EDITION

Manufactured in the United States of America

Library of Congress Cataloging in Publication Data
Main entry under title:

The Complete guide to blacksmithing.

Reprint. Originally published: Chicago: M.A.
Donohue, 1902.
    1. Blacksmithing. 2. Horseshoeing. 3. Carriage
and wagon making. I. Lungwitz, A. (Anton), 1845-
Lehrmeister im Hufbeschlag. II. Adams, Charles F.
TT220.C67 1981   682   81-3846
ISBN 0-517-34548-X   AACR2

CONTENTS.

PART I.

GENERAL BLACKSMITHING.

PART II.

HORSESHOEING.

Contents.

Part III.

CARRIAGE BUILDING.

LIST OF ILLUSTRATIONS.

List of Illustrations.

FOREWORD.

Many old crafts, with intrinsic techniques that were handed down from father to son, died with the men who practiced them. As society industrialized and specialists emerged, it was no longer necessary for a person to be a Renaissance man. Only lately have we begun to unwind the threads leading back in time to tap the experience and knowledge of our parents and grandparents. Only lately have we taken time from our busy leaps into technology to understand that previous generations were quite competent and able to do many things for themselves—things that many of us have not attempted to tackle lest they be "too difficult" and "only something learned by long practice" by people who "know what they're doing."

Today, a pervasive attitude is "if someone else can do it, so can I." Individuals are searching for answers to problems in fields totally out of their experience.

Ironworking is one of those fields. It's a craft that almost fell into oblivion, but its rescue has been accomplished. Blacksmith societies are flourishing throughout the world. The people who are

responsible are digging into, studying, and trea-
suring the infinite range and styles of objects
made by the unsung creators of the past. They are
almost legendary people who laboriously pumped
the bellows that fanned the fires to heat the forges
and who have left a rich heritage, despite their
anonymity.

Fortunately, some of that heritage has not been
lost to ashes and dust. Blacksmithing has a language of its own. If we could gather together
smiths from every century, they could communi-
cate with one another through the language of the
hammer on the metal. Unable to do that, the re-
printing of Professor Lungwitz's book recaptures
much of that discourse. First printed in 1902, *The
Complete Guide to Blacksmithing* provides information known when smithing was a flowering
craft used to create essentials of everyday life,
from horseshoes to ornate carriages.

When a book such as this surfaces eighty years
later, one can again experience nostalgia, if so
inclined. Those who love the smell of the smoke,
the rhythmic clang of the hammer on the anvil, the
glow of the embers, and the romance of the old
handmade object, will appreciate the information
in this book.

Whether you want to restore an old wagon or to
create a modern gate or chandelier, you will dis-

cover hundreds of hints for working with metals.
If you are a hobbyist blacksmith, who snatches
forge time in a garage, a makeshift shed, or in the
great outdoors—without benefit of a neighbor's
experience—you may find answers that have been
unavailable elsewhere. Much of the information is
unique. All of it is useful.

Dona Z. Meilach
1981

PUBLISHERS' PREFACE.

Without doubt the most thoroughly reliable handbook of horseshoeing is the German text-book of Professor Lungwitz, director of the Shoeing School of the Royal Veterinary College at Dresden. The conditions in Germany are almost identical with those in this country, and the Shoeing School superintended by Professor Lungwitz may safely be regarded as the best in the world. Certainly there is none like it in the United States.

But Professor Lungwitz's discussion of the anatomy of the horse's foot is too technical for the ordinary reader, and his book gives no suggestions on the elementary principles of blacksmithing, which are prerequisites of any attempt at shoeing a horse. To make the present handbook complete, these directions have been added, and the text of Professor Lungwitz's book has been somewhat condensed and simplified. Moreover, a chapter on carriage-ironing, with other general information, has been added,

that the manual may be thoroughly practical and as complete as possible.

It is certainly true that every owner and
driver of horses, as well as every person who
professes to be a horseshoer, should have a
thorough knowledge of the horse's foot and
the requirements in the way of shoeing. But
how many do! Even farriers know no more
of the horse's hoof, and the scientific requirements for obtaining the best results in any given
case, than they have been able to pick up in
the exercise of their trade. This kind of knowledge is notoriously imperfect. It will never
improve. And owners and drivers are for the
most part so ignorant that they could not tell
a front foot from a hind foot, or tell the difference between a job of shoeing that would make
a horse lame in a week, and one that would cure
the same lameness in even less time. And
this ignorance costs the owner many a hard-
earned dollar. No better investment can be
made than a little time spent in the study of
the horse's feet, by the help of a really scientific
manual. But it is better not to study any book
at all than one that is unreliable.

It is believed that the present volume will
meet the popular need better than any other that
has yet been issued. The authoritativeness

of anything from the pens of Professor Lungwitz and Mr. Adams is unimpeachable, while the publishers have given the volume a practical character which must inevitably appeal to the common sense of the average reader.

PART I.

GENERAL BLACKSMITHING.

CHAPTER I.

THE FORGE.

The Forge and Blast. This is the term usually applied to the blacksmith's open fire or hearth, where iron is heated by agency of a blast. Fig. 1 shows an elevation of a form of hearth very common in this country. When of the largest size, this hearth is a kind of trough of brickwork, about six feet square, elevated several inches from the floor of the shop. One side is extended into a vertical wall leading to the chimney, the lower end of which terminates in a head, or hood of stout iron plates which catch the smoke from the open hearth and guide it to the chimney. The back wall of the forge is provided with a thick cast iron plate, level with the hearth. This is called the "back," and has in its centre a thick projecting

11

iron nozzle, perforated to allow the wind for the blast to pass into the forge.   This is termed the "tue" or "tuyere," French for a tube or pipe.   The large leathern bellows which supply the blast are either actuated by a long handle, or worked by a treadle as shown in the figure.

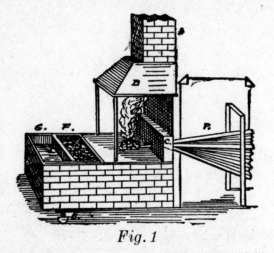

Fig. 1

The bellows should be double, that is, divided by a horizontal partition, which separates the entire bellows into a working or under part, and a regulating or upper part.   By lowering the under part after it has been raised, the valve in its bottom will be forced open by the pressure of the atmosphere, and the lower compartment will fill with air.   On raising the bottom, the lower valve closes, and the air in the under part is compressed and forced through the valve in the partition, whence the weight of the top drives it through the tuyere or nozzle. The pressure may be increased by putting weights upon the top. The bellows may be driven by machinery or power, where such can be procured, quite as well as by hand.

Many prefer the circular bellows, or the fan; and in large smithies air is supplied to a vast number of forges through pipes fed by air-pumps.

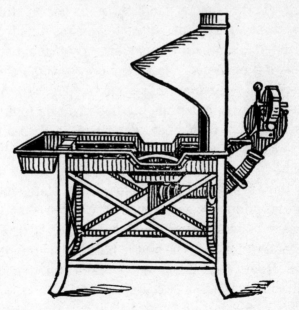

Fig. 2

Fig. 2 shows a steel portable forge, composed entirely of iron and steel, with a fan worked by a crank, the air-pipe passing downward and through a "tuyere" into the coal-box.

In front of the hearth are usually two plate-iron troughs, one to contain coal, the other (the slake trough) being filled with water.

The tuyere or tue iron is generally a simple block of cast iron six or eight inches long and three inches square, with a tapered bore of one inch at the smaller and three inches at the larger end.   The narrow part, which is directed to the fire, can be made narrower by placing an iron ring of more or less thickness within the aperture.   Tuyeres have been contrived of various forms, but probably none will be found superior to that just described.   Hot-air tuyeres have been used, but are now generally abandoned.   The water tuyere is, on account of its durability, very valuable.   Here the cast iron forge back is made hollow so that a stream of water may circulate through it from a small cistern.   The water back is, therefore, kept from becoming intensely hot, and it and the tuyere last much longer.

The Spring Bellows.   A noted smith says, "Of all the bellows that I have seen or used, one with the spring attached beats them all

for a steady blast. You would be surprised
to see the difference there is in the blast of
these bellows when the spring is used and when
it is not. A, in Fig. 3, is the spring which is
bolted on to the piece B, with three carriage

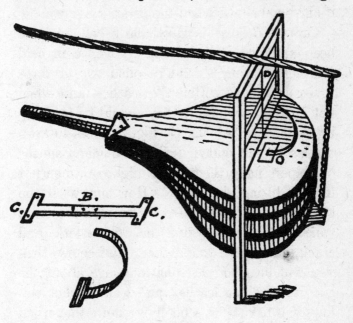

Fig. 3

bolts; then the ends CC are fastened to the
two posts XX. This shows spring applied
ready for use. At O there is a square plate
fastened to the bellows with four screws; this
plate keeps the spring from wearing in the top

board of the bellows. The spring A is made from a piece of 1 by ¼ inch spring steel, the crossbar B was made from an old tire, but could be made of wood. In fastening the spring to the posts XX, leave about ½-inch space between it and the bellows when the bellows is down."

Care of Bellows. How many bellows have been and are spoiled from negligence in cold weather? They should be oiled two or three times a year to soften the leather, and when not in use (over night) they should be hung up by a chain as per line D (Fig. 3) so as to keep the leather distended. But how many smiths or helpers hang them up at night or when not in use during the day? How many oil the bellows at all? On a cold winter's morning, start your fire and give the pole a jerk, and crack, crack goes the leather. Of course then you will hear some strong language about the good-for-nothing leather, and what a poor bellows you have. A schoolboy knows that when leather is dry it will break like chips. So, clean and oil your bellows before the cold weather comes on.

The Anvil. The tool next in importance to the forge is the anvil (Fig. 4). This is not only of interest as a tool of the trade, but it requires some investigation, since the steeling of the anvil is a matter of importance. Anvils for •heavy work are generally square blocks of iron, with steel faces. In many instances, however, it is merely a cast iron block with chilled face. The common smith's anvil is made entirely of wrought iron, and the upper part or face is covered with hardened steel. The making of an anvil is heavy work, as the whole of it is

Fig. 4

performed by hand. Anvils vary in weight from less than one hundred pounds to over five hundred. For their manufacture two large fires are required. The principal portion, or core of the anvil—a large square block of iron— is heated to the welding heat at a certain point or corner in one of the fires, and the piece of iron that is to form a projcting end is heated at another fire. When the core and the corner have both reached the welding heat, they are wrought together upon an anvil and joined by heavy swing hammers. In this way the four corners of the base are welded to the body in four heats. After this the projection for the shank hole, and lastly the beak, are welded to the core. The whole is then wrought into a proper shape by paring and trimming for the reception of the face. The steel used for this purpose is, or ought to be, the best kind of sheer steel; blistered steel is, however, frequently substituted. The anvil and steel are heated in different fires until they attain the proper temperature. The two sides which are to be welded are then sprinkled with calcined borax and joined by quickly repeated blows of the hand hammer. The steel generally used is half an inch thick; but if it is only a quarter of an inch in thickness the difference is unimportant if the steel be good. Steel of an inferior quality if too thick is apt to fly or crack in hardening.

The steeled anvil is next heated to redness, and brought under a fall of water of at least the size of its face and of three or four feet head. After hardening, it is smoothed upon a grindstone, and finally polished with emery. Small anvils such as are used by silversmiths are polished with a crocus and have a mirror-like face.

The expensiveness of wrought iron anvils has induced their manufacture of cast iron. The common anvil, however, cannot be made of cast iron, for the beak would not be strong enough. None but anvils with full square faces have been successfully made of cast iron. These have either been simply chilled by casting the faces in iron molds, or the face is plated with cast steel. Chilled cast iron anvils are not much in use. They are too brittle and the corners of the face will not stand. Cast iron anvils with cast-steel faces, however, are a superior article and in many respects preferable to wrought iron. The face is harder and stronger, though the beaks will not last as long. For purposes where a good face is essential, as for copper and tin smiths, the cast iron anvil with cast steel face will be found to answer every purpose.

The anvil is generally set upon the butt-end of a large block of wood, oak being preferred. It is placed loosely upon it, being secured merely by a few spikes or wedges driven into the wood. Cutlers, filemakers, and those who manufacture small articles of steel, place their anvils upon blocks of stone, in order to make their foundation firm, preventing recoil, and giving efficiency to light but quick blows with the hammer.

In working soft metals, such as copper and its compounds, a layer of felt between the anvil and the block will be found of advantage.   The anvils upon which steel articles are to be forged are generally fashioned at the bottom in the form of cubes, for insertion by means of wedges either in stone or wooden stocks.   A black-smith's anvil, on the contrary, is formed with projecting corner bases, which are bolted down to the stock.

The Hammer.   Second only to the anvil among smiths' tools comes the hammer.   Primitive man must have needed and used rude stone hammers, such as are often unearthed at the present day.   These ancient stone hammers had usually a groove round them for the handle, which was probably of supple withes.

The more usual form of the ordinary smiths' hammer generally weighs from one to two pounds.   Sometimes the handle is nearer to the "pane" or narrow end, the broad end being known as the "face."   The ordinary smiths' sledge weighs from five to eight pounds. A heavy sledge weighs from twelve to fifteen pounds, and a swing sledge from twenty-five to thirty pounds.   Cutlers and edge-tool makers generally prefer a hammer with the handle near the pane side.   The uphand sledge is used for comparatively light work. The swing or "about" sledge is grasped by both hands at the extremity of the handle, and swung at arm's length over the head, giving the heaviest possible blow of which a hand-hammer is capable.

There are two forms of the ordinary clip-

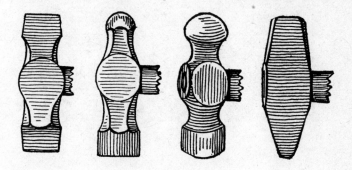

Fig. 5

ping hammer (Fig. 5), either with the pane parallel with the handle as shown in the upper figure, or with a ball pane or a pane elongated at right angles with the handle. The pane is mostly used for riveting, and it is quite a question which is the best form. The hammer is one of these tools that the workman gets used to, and "gets the hang of," and there is a good deal in this term as applied to a hammer, as will be seen presently.

It takes about a year to get thoroughly at

home with either after having become accustomed to the other or either of them.

We now come to the proper shape for the eye, to enable it to hold the hammer firmly

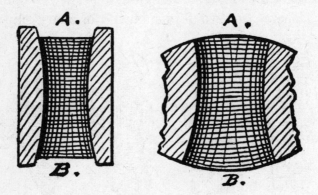

Fig. 6

and not in time get loose. The best form is that shown in Fig. 6, the handle end or bottom of the eye being rounded out as at B, and the top being rounded across the hammer, but not lengthwise. The rounding out prevents the handle from getting too far through the eye, and when the eye is wedged at the top with a single wedge, the spread across the eye prevents the handle from coming loose. This locks the handle firmly, while requiring one wedge only. A wooden wedge is preferable to an iron one, providing the handle and the wedge are of dry, well seasoned wood.

The Tongs. These constitute a very indispensable class of tools in the smithy. One of the most useful kinds of modern tongs is known as the "flat-bit" tongs (Fig. 7 A). They vary in size from one to five feet in length, and from half a pound to ten pounds in weight. The fire end is made to fit very close for thin work, or to stand more open for thick work, but always parallel. An oval coupler or iron ring is usually put upon the "reins" or shanks of the tongs to keep their hold upon the work (as seen in Fig. 7).

Fig. 7

Next in general utility are the pincer tongs (Fig. 7B). These are sometimes made with hollow, half round bits; but it is better that the bits be angular, as they are then equally useful for round rods or for square bars held at opposite angles.   When the bits of these tongs are made long and bowed behind they are extremely useful for holding bolts, etc., the heads of which can be placed in the hollow portion.

These two varieties of tongs will serve most purposes.

Other Tools.   Among the numerous other tools that prove useful to the blacksmith are punches and chisels (which may be held by twisted hazel rods or tongs); "top and bottom tools,"used in pairs, one being set in the anvil (the top and bottom "fullers" are used for grooving in the hot iron around a horseshoe); the set "hammer,"a small tool held against the hot iron while its top is struck with the hammer, thus rendering the blow more certain than if made direct by the hammer; and "heading" tools, employed in forging for swaging heads on stems of bolts.   Swages are of great utility. They consist of tools having certain definite shapes, so that the hot iron, being placed in or below them, takes their shape when struck. Sometimes they are used in pairs and sometimes singly.

All smiths' tools are faced with steel, and would in fact be cheaper in the end if they were wholly made of that metal. Tongs made of spring steel are by far the best in the end, although costing more in the first instance. Tools should never be heated red hot, and when they have to be brought into contact with heated iron they should be frequently cooled. Tools are held by hazel rods soaked in water and twisted to prevent hurting the hand by the blow of the hammer.

CHAPTER II.

The Fire. The coal employed in the smith's forge is usually bituminous, anthracite not being adapted to the purpose. No coals with metallic mixtures are suitable, because these are generally marked by the presence of sulphur also, which is very detrimental. Charcoal may be substituted for coal.

The smith's fire may be made either open or hollow, the latter being generally preferred.

When about to light his fire, the smith scrapes back the cinders and removes the used ashes or slack to the ashpit. Some wood shavings are then placed upon the nozzle of the tuyere and lighted. When these are burning low the cinders are raked back over them and the bellows are set to work. In a short time a white smoke rises, shortly afterward followed by tongues of flame breaking forth. A thin poker is now cautiously introduced as far as the tuyere. Next the work is placed in the fire, and fresh coal is laid on and over the fire and patted down with the fire shovel. As the process goes on, fresh coal is continually added to the margin of the fire and pushed forward into the heart of it as is required.

In large hollow fires, after a tolerable fire has been obtained by lighting in the usual manner, the live coal is drawn forward on the hearth so as to expose the aperture of the tuyere. A suitable sized piece of iron (or the poker) is put into this aperture. Small coal well wetted is now placed round this iron and well beaten together into a mass termed the " stock," the length of which from the tuyere nozzle is regulated by the distance which it is desired the fire should stand off from the tuyere. Then more small coal is heaped up for a second stock opposite the first, but farther out on the hearth. These stocks should both be well beaten down which is sometimes aided by the sledge hammer. The iron which was inserted in the tuyere is drawn out before the second hill of stock is built up, leaving a hole for the tuyere pipe. The two heaps of stock appear with a gap between them where the fire lies. Into this gap or hollow space the weld is laid, covered over with two or three pieces of wood and a heap of wetted coal carefully banked over it and beaten down by the shovel. A gentle blast is kept up while these operations are going on, and the work is not taken out till the pieces of wood are consumed and the flames penetrate the coals at each end, when the work can be taken out without fear of disfiguring the fire. The instrument generally employed to wet the coal is a bundle of straw passed lightly through an iron ring formed at the end of a rod and kept in the slake trough. Damp, slack coal is thrown on the fire in a layer two or three inches thick. It will cake together, and after the loose coal is burned out, form a hollow fire, the coke roof reflecting an intense heat on the material beneath it. By no other means can a fire be made to possess so intense a heat as by the method we have described.

Flux. Sand or other material sprinkled upon iron when near the welding heat serves to form a flux or fluid glass with the iron. This flux surrounds the hot iron or steel and protects it against the impurities of the fuel, removing at the same time the coating of dry scales from the heated metals and greatly facilitating the operation of welding.

For welding steel to steel and steel to iron, we have a variety of degrees of heat to deal with and the flux which serves to protect iron is insufficient to protect cast steel, just as, on the other hand, the flux which fits cast steel for welding would be useless on iron. Impure wrought iron will form a slag of its own material, while good iron is protected, as we have intimated above, by sprinkling fine sand over it. But this method will not answer with steel, or where steel and iron are to be welded. For welding iron, clean river sand, or powdered sandstone, make a good flux; for steel, borax is generally used. With common brine, clay makes a very fine flux and clean surface to which steel readily adheres. The material to be used as a flux is to be applied shortly before the metal reaches the welding heat, no matter how high or low that heat may be. It will melt on the surface of the iron. Borax in crystals as commonly sold is composed of nearly one half water. On heating these crystals in an iron pot they dissolve into a clear liquid. On heating further, the water is evaporated and the residuum resumes the appearance of a spongy mass, and by the continued application of heat this mass is converted into a clear glass. This glass is what is called calcined borax. It is entirely free from water and not very likely to absorb it. It should be prepared and powdered in advance, and be always on hand for use. Borax thus prepared is sufficient in nearly all cases. Still, some work-

ers in steel prefer a mixture of two parts borax
with one of sal-ammoniac, or three parts of the
former with one of the latter article.   This com-
pound is preferable for welding iron and steel.
Borax alone is rather too liquid for iron.   Where
it is to be welded to steel, a more efficient flux
is well-dried and finely-powdered potters' clay—
not common loam—which has been moistened
with salt water; and it lasts long enough to be
brought to the anvil for welding.

The slag flows off or is forced out in bringing
the two surfaces together and pressing them
into close contact.   If iron or steel is heated in
contact with air, it burns and forms a film of
infusible magnetic oxide, the metals cannot come
fairly into contact, and of course the welding is
imperfect.   It cannot be sound.   After the flux
is strewn on the iron, it is necessary to turn the
metal constantly in the fire, otherwise the flux
will flow to the lower parts and finally be lost.
A better method than that of sprinkling the sand
on the hot iron is to roll the metal in the powdered flux, thus saving the latter and keeping
the fire more free from clinkers.

We do not advise mixing the sal-ammoniac
with borax, as the ammonia has a tendency to
convert the steel into iron.   If pure borax is too
refractory, as is the case with some of the best

kinds of steel, an excellent flux may be produced by melting potash, or pearlash, together with pure dried clay, three parts of the former and one of the latter, in an iron pot; adding to the fluid mass gradually an equal weight of calcined borax. This flux should be finely powdered and used like the borax. It melts at a dark brown heat, vitrifying the iron slag perfectly, and is not injurious to steel. This metal rapidly deteriorates in quality if the atmosphere has access to it while hot. A suitable flux, therefore, which protects it, and at the same time purifies the surface, is all important.

Degrees of Heat. In all kinds of forging the iron or steel must be heated in the forge to a greater or less degree of heat in order to lessen the cohesion of its particles and render it more malleable and pliable as well as more ready to enter into cohesion with the particles of another similarly heated piece when exposed to the blows of the hammer.

"Pure iron," says Holtzappel, "will bear an almost unlimited degree of heat, the hot-short iron will bear much less, and is in fact very brittle when heated; and of steel, the shear steel will generally bear the highest temperature, the blistered steel the next, and cast steel the least of all; but all these kinds, and especially the cast steel, differ very much according to the process of manufacture."

That iron is the best, all things being equal, which will bear the highest degree of heat. The usual degrees of temperature recognized are five, viz.:

The black heat, just visible by daylight;

The low red or cherry red heat, appearing crimson in daylight;

The bright red or bright cherry red heat, in which the black scales can be seen and look black;

The white heat, when the scales are hardly visible, or the scales and iron are nearly the same color;

The welding heat, when the iron begins to burn with vivid sparks.

The latter heat is very variable, pure fibrous iron sustaining almost any degree of heat so long as it is protected by a slag.

Steel does not bear the same degree of heat without injury. The finest cast steel will hardly sustain a bright red heat without falling to pieces, rendering it imprudent to heat it higher than a middling or cherry red. Blistered steel will resist a far higher degree of heat than cast steel, and good shear steel will endure a white heat without much injury. German steel can be heated to the welding heat of good iron. Although very sensitive to heat, steel will bear much more forging than iron, if not previously injured by too great a heat.

In forging steel, no heavy tools, at least no heavy sledge, should be used. A good-sized hammer with a rapid succession of strokes will be sufficient. This is, in fact, the best method of forging steel.

Iron is usually worked at the cherry red or white heat, the welding heat being alone reached in cases where that operation is to be performed. As, however, the working of the iron tends to separate its fibres, it is sometimes brought to the welding heat and well hammered to ensure their reunion.

When iron is heated to a dull red heat its defects and cracks become very visible, and this expedient is frequently resorted to to test or examine doubtful forgings.

When it is requisite that a forging be specially sound, it is not uncommon to heat it and work it well under the hammer. This process, which is an imitation of that sustained in the original manufacture, is termed "taking a heat over it." The "heat" is generally understood to mean a welding heat.

The use of the sand, as we have already men-

tioned, is to preserve the surface of the heated
metal from oxidization, which would prevent the
union of the metal.   When the sand is sprinkled
on red hot iron it falls off, but when on iron at
the welding heat it fuses and covers the face of
the iron with a vitreous or glassy glaze, which
protects it from contact with the air.   When
this point of heat has been slightly exceeded,
the iron begins to burn and throw off a shower
of vivid sparks, hissing sharply, meanwhile; in
fact, it looks like a snowball, as smiths sometimes say.

When two pieces of iron are to be welded
together,it is essential that both reach the proper
heat at the same moment.   This must be man-
aged by arranging them in the fire in a suitable
manner.   The most intensely heating part of
the fire is, of course, opposite the tuyere or
blast, and the most backward piece is put there.
In all cases it is necessary to allow sufficient
time for the heat to soak in, as it were.   If the
blast is urged too rapidly or forcibly, the outside of the iron may be burned away (especially
if the piece be large) before the centre has exceeded a red heat.   The heating should proceed
smoothly and gradually.

As the work cools it is not well to continue
the hammering which is intended to leave a

smooth surface too long, as this may stretch the outer surface more than the inner part, and actually cause them to separate, leaving the outer part quite distinct, as the bark of a tree from its trunk. This has often been noticed when bad forgings have been examined. Hence the finishing, or "battering off" as it is technically termed, should not be continued too long.

Drawing Down. This is the usual term for reducing the work. When the iron is to be thinned in substance and expanded both in length and breadth, the flat face of the hammer is brought to bear upon it when at the proper heat. If, however, it is to be stretched only one way — either in length or breadth — the pane of the hammer may be employed at right angles to the direction in which the extension is desired. Hammers are made with panes in different directions for this purpose. Set hammers are also used, being placed on the work and their tops struck with the sledge. Tools of this kind with very wide faces are sometimes called "flatters," and "fullers" are also employed for this kind of work.

When the object to be drawn down, say a square bar, is to have its sides kept parallel, the flat face of the hammer is used, and great

care must be taken that it fall parallel to the
anvil. If the object under the hammer be a
square bar, it should be turned a quarter round
at each stroke, which, if done accurately, will
draw down the bar perfectly square.

The art of thus twisting the work a quarter
round is difficult to acquire, and the early efforts
of the young smith are almost sure to have a
lozenge or diamond shaped section; but when
the knack is once acquired, it is astonishing how
true the smith will keep his work. He seems
to secure its squareness almost by instinct. Of
course bar iron, originally square, helps to ensure the object, as only two sides of a square
object need to be exposed to the hammer stroke,
their opposite parallel sides being similarlystruck
by the anvil upon the well-known principle of
mechanics, that action and reaction are equal.

The smith usually holds the work or tongs
lightly, not with too constrained a grasp, and
allows the hammer to fall perfectly flat and in
the centre of the bar. It is good practice for
the young smith to hammer a bar of cold iron
or steel and observe the indentations afterwards.
If he do not bring down his hammer flat, the
marks on the bar will soon tell their tale.

We will now suppose that the smith wishes
to draw down to a point six inches of the end

of a bar for a tongue or otherwise. When sufficiently hot, the iron bar is taken from the fire and rested over the farther side of the anvil, where the smith strikes it and turns it a quarter round. He then gradually draws it toward him, striking it each time he makes the quarter turn, until he finishes off at the point.

In smoothing off the work, the hammer is brought down at one spot on the centre of the anvil with the face parallel, and the work is gradually brought under it.

In using the chisel or punch, the hazel withe well soaked in water is to be preferred as a handle as it prevents the jar from hurting the hand. When the anvil chisel has been set in the hole in the anvil and used for cutting off a piece of iron the blows should be made gradually lighter and lighter as the cutting is nearly completed. In the use of the punch, especially if the piece of iron worked is thick, care should be taken that the punch does not stick to the iron. To prevent this, a little coal dust may be sprinkled in the hole. When the punch gets red hot it should be immediately cooled off.

Set-off. A set-off is a reduction from the original size of the bar with a square shoulder or two square shoulders. For this, the part where the shoulder is to be is placed at the edge of the anvil, and then struck with the hammer. When two shoulders are to be made, the work may be held at the edge of the anvil, and a set hammer held in the proper position and struck. This "sets" the upper shoulder, the lower one being made by the anvil.

Note that the edges of the set hammer, etc., should not be too sharp, as they act partially as chisels and injure the work. There is no danger of this with the round-ended fullers, which can be used in drawing down where a top and bottom fuller are both employed. This latter tool is also very handy when iron is to be set off and extended laterally. Here the iron may first be nicked across with the fuller, and then spread out, the indentations being afterward smoothed off with the hammer.

Jumping or Upsetting. This process is usually resorted to when it is required to render the iron bar or whatever it may be a little thicker at some portion of its length, yet not so much as to necessitate welding a collar on. For instance, if the portion to be checked is at the extreme end, a "short heat" is taken; that is to say, the extreme end is made white hot, and instantly thrust down or "jumped" several times upon the anvil; or it is stood upon the anvil with the cold end uppermost, and the lat-

ter is struck forcibly with a hammer until
the desired effect is produced at the heated end.
This makes a burr at the end suitable for turning
up into a head. When the heat is taken at a
point distant from the end, the same procedure
should be taken. Should the heat have been
taken too "long"—that is, too much of the iron
have been heated—the adjacent portions should
be cooled down before the bar is "jumped."

Shutting Together. This is the welding of two
pieces of bar or rod together, sometimes called
"shutting up." The simplest way of doing this
is to bring the ends to the form of a "scarf"
(which is of much the same form as a carpenter's
scarf in wood). Each piece is then brought to
a welding heat, and a little sand strewed on
each. The smith then takes one piece, and his
assistant the other, placing them in position,
and the fireman then gives two or three blows
with his hammer, which unites them. The
assistant striker or smiter then joins in with
his sledge, and both hammers are kept swiftly
in operation until the work is finished. The
smith "jumps" the joint on the anvil before
finally leaving it, both to test the soundness of
the joint and to thicken the iron at the place
in case the forging should have drawn it down

a little.   The scarfs, or flat edges, are bevelled
to render their union more easy.

In ordinary light work, the sledge hammer is
generally used "uphand," that is to say, the
right hand is slid up the handle toward the head
as the tool is lifted, and slipped down again as
it descends.   "About sledge" signifies that the
striker is to swing the sledge in a circle between
each blow, when his hands slide down to the
end of the handle and the blow is much heavier.
When the fireman wishes his assistant to dis-
continue striking, it is usually the custom for
him to tap the anvil with his own hammer.
The double or alternate hammering between the
forger or fireman and hammerman should at
first be gently done, to avoid danger to the arm
from not holding the work level on the anvil.
The hammerman should first begin and strike
at the rate of one blow a second; after a few
blows the smith begins, and both hammer the
work at times, and at other times the anvil.

Great care should be taken that no coal dust
gets on the surfaces to be welded, or the joint
will certainly be spoiled.

This scarf joint, just described, is the almost
universal method of uniting two small pieces of
iron, whether square, round, or flat.   In large
pieces one end is generally drawn down and the

Fig. 8

other cleft (Fig. 8), or the ends are made to fit
each other square, a shallow slot made in each
and an iron tongue (called a charlin or stick-in
piece) laid in (Fig. 9). The first operation is

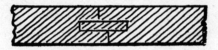

Fig. 9

the tongue or split joint, the second the butt
joint, because the ends abut on each other. In
either case the ends are brought together in the
fire; the proper heat being attained, the joint
is jumped together by the end of each piece
being struck by heavy sledge hammers, the
heat being meanwhile kept up. Lastly, the
work is taken to the anvil and finished there.

Fig. 10 shows the T joint. In the first cut
the transverse bar is thinned down at this junction and the other chamfered or bevelled. When
the T is made of thick iron, it is well to upset

the end of the stem piece and mold it with the
fuller to something the shape of the letter T.
A heat of both pieces is then taken and the full-
ered piece is welded to the bar, as shown.

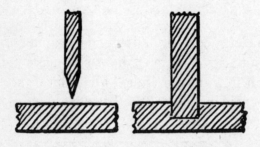

Fig. 10

Hardening Steel. The hardening of steel is
an operation which requires the exercise of some
judgment. The usual method is to heat the
steel to a certain point and then plunge it suddenly into cold water, tempering it afterwards.
This method is undoubtedly the correct one;
but the degree of heat to which the steel is to
be exposed before cooling is a matter of vast importance. Some steel—the natural, for instance
—will bear a strong white heat and a plunge
into cold water before it assumes its greatest
hardness. Other steels, particularly the fine
cast steel, will not bear more than a brown or
cherry red heat; beyond that point it burns

and becomes brittle in hardening. It may safely be concluded that steel that does not bear heat in forging will not bear it in hardening The heat at which steel falls to pieces or melts is too high for hardening, as steel hardened in such a heat will fly or crack. The alterations manifest in steel after hardening, as compared with annealed steel, are the following: Its volume is a little increased; the black scales which adhere to its surface fly off, and the surface appears clean, and of the color and lustre of iron; the fracture is brighter, and crystals are visible. Good steel as we have said before, is silver-white, and is so hard that it will scratch pane glass, and even a file. The cohesion, relative and absolute, is increased if the heat has not been too high before cooling. These are the chief characteristics of good steel when hardened.

It is not possible to give any distinguishing mark between steel, wrought iron, and cast iron. As a general feature, however, we may say that cast iron cannot be forged or welded, or at least very perfectly; that wrought iron feels softer under the hammer than steel in forging; and that both impure wrought and cast iron become very brittle in hardening. The united hardness and tenacity of steel are its chief characteristics. Good cast steel, or any other variety, if not freshly annealed or hardened, and if free from fissures, will emit a sonorous, silvery tone when a suspended bar is struck. Iron, particularly if good, emits a dull leaden sound, while cast iron gives out a tone like that of a cracked instrument.

The surest test of the quality of steel is to draw a rod into a tapered point, harden it by a gentle heat, and break off pieces from the point. The degree of resistance to the hammer, which of course should be a very small one, is the test of the value of the steel. The best steel is that which, under this treatment, is found to be toughest and strongest.

Case-Hardening is that process by which the surface of iron is converted into steel. In this process the surface of the iron may be made harder than the finest steel and still retain all its toughness and malleability.

The articles to be case-hardened are to be well polished, and if the iron is not quite sound, or shows ash-holes, it is hammered over and polished again—the finer the polish the better. The articles are then embedded in coarse charcoal powder in a wrought iron box or pipe, which should be air tight. A pipe is preferable, because it can be turned and the heat applied more uniformly. The whole is then exposed for twenty-four hours to a gentle cherry-red heat in the flue of a steam boiler, or in some other place where the heat is uniformly kept up. This makes a very hard surface, and, on large objects, one-eighth of an inch in depth may be obtained. If so much time cannot be given to the operation, and no deep hardening is required, the articles are embedded in animal charcoal, or in a mixture of animal and coal. Four or five hours, heat will make a good surface of steel. If a single article, such as a small key or other tool, is to be hardened, the coal must be finely pulverized and mixed into a paste with a saturated solution of salt: with this paste the iron is well covered and dried. Over the paste is laid a coating of clay, moistened with salt water, which is also gently dried. The whole is now exposed to a gradually increasing heat up to a bright red, but not beyond it. This will give a fine surface to small objects. In all cases the article is plunged into cold water when heated the proper time and up to a proper degree.

A quick mode of case-hardening small objects is to polish them well and heat to a dark red heat; then roll in the powder of yellow prussiate of potash, and sprinkle the powder over. The powder will melt on the surface, and the iron is then heated to a bright red and plunged into cold water. The powder is obtained from the crystal of prussiate of potash by gently heating in an open pot to drive off the water. The remaining powder is white. Close-fibred pure iron should be selected.

For hardening, always use pure well water fresh and cool from the well.

PART II.

HORSESHOEING.

CHAPTER I.

THE ANATOMY OF THE HORSE'S FOOT.

It is evident that no intelligent work can be done in shoeing a horse unless the structure and method of growth of the foot are entirely

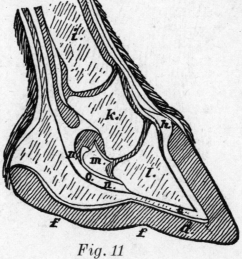

Fig. 11

47

familiar. Professor Lungwitz in his German text-book devotes considerable space to a technical and somewhat full study of the anatomy of the horse's foot—a study of course necessary for all scientific students who must pass a government examination. The present edition is

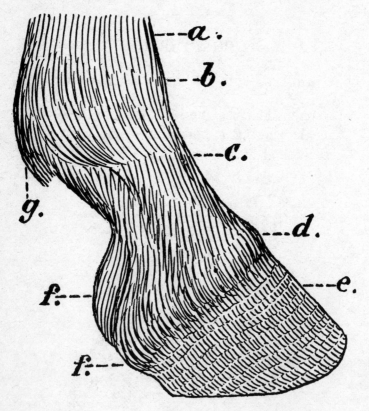

Fig. 12

intended for the common reader and not the scientific special student, however, and a simpler exposition of the subject has been chosen.

The best way to study the structure of a horse's foot is to get the foot of a dead horse and soak it in water for a week or two, when it may easily be taken apart. When the hard outer shell has been removed, the sensitive inner foot may be dissected by the aid of a sharp knife.

By comparing Figs. 11 and 12 we may get a good idea of the general structure of the foot. In Fig. 11 the fetlock joint where the cannon-bone meets the long pastern is not shown, as in Fig. 12, where the cannon-bone is indicated by A, the fetlock joint by B, and the long pastern by C. This is the bone which appears in Fig. 11 as I.

The hoof is not solid, though it appears so from the outside. What we see is the hard outer wall or crust AA (Fig. 11). Beneath that are the insensitive laminae, or leaves, BB, next to which, lying against the bone, are the sensitive laminae CC, which are a mass of nerves and blood-vessels. There is an insensitive sole, D, which is a kind of horny substance, and the insensitive frog FF. Above these lie the sensitive sole E and the sensitive frog G. The prin-

cipal bones of the foot are four in number, I
the long pastern, K the short pastern, L the
coffin bone, and M the navicular bone, over
which as a fulcrum works the flexor perforans
tendon NN. O marks the seat of navicular
disease.

The Hoof in General. The hoof is not absolutely regular in form, and each of the four feet
shows some peculiarity by which it is possible
to tell at a glance whether it is a fore foot or a
hind, a right or a left.

The fore feet are less pointed at the toe than
the hind, but more sloping. The two fore feet
and the two hind should be evenly balanced
and nearly alike. The right hoof is distinguished
from the left by the fact that the outer border
is higher and more prominent, while the inner
is more upright.

The Wall. This is the hard outer horn with
which the horseshoer has most to do. It is
more sloping in front than at the sides, and at
the back it turns in on itself to form the heels.
The turned in portions on either side the frog
are called the *bars*. The general shape of a fore
foot viewed from the bottom may be seen in
Fig. 13. It will be seen that the turned in portions of the wall form the bars at a sharp angle.

Externally the wall is hard and smooth, being

covered by a varnish-like coating, often marked
by rings. On the inner side it is softer and
more elastic, and presents various irregularities
of surface (horny leaves) corresponding to the
irregularities in the surface of the sensitive hoof.

Fig. 13

It is most elastic at the upper edge, in which on
the inner side is the coronary groove, into which
fits the coronary band of which we shall speak
presently. The lower edge is called the bearing
or plantar edge, as the weight of the horse falls
upon this portion, and it is to this that the shoe
is fixed.

The thickness of the wall is variable. In front feet it is thickest at the toe, and becomes thinner toward the heels. In general, the most slanting portion is always the thickest. The thickness varies at the toe from three to five eighths of an inch, and at the heels from one to two fifths of an inch.

The wall consists of three layers, the outer layer, a thin varnish-like covering that is very hard, the middle layer which is thickest and strongest, and the inner layer lying in parallel horn leaves corresponding to the surface of the sensitive hoof. This inner layer is always white, even when the rest of the hoof is dark.

The Sole. The horn sole is about as thick as the wall, covering the bottom of the foot and curving upward into a hollow of the coffin bone. It does not touch the ground ordinarily, and the lower side is rough and often covered with loose scales of dead horn which peel off of themselves and fall away. The upper side is covered with velvet-like tissue which secretes the horn that goes to form the hard sole.

The White Line marking the junction of the sole and the wall, is formed by the inner layer of the wall, which we have spoken of as composed of horn leaves that are always white. This white line may be traced all around the hoof and even up along the bars to the frog and is soft and crumbling, so that in places it may disappear. Usually it is of a dirty white color, due to discoloration from manure, dirt, and iron rust. It is very important, as it shows the thickness of the wall, and marks the line to which the horseshoe nails should penetrate.

The Frog. This portion of the sole is a projecting horny formation lying on a thick fleshy cushion from which it is secreted. The frog lies as a wedge between the outer edges of the bars or turned in portion of the hoof, with both of which it is united. The horn is very soft and elastic, and is divided into two portions by the cleft in its middle. On the upper side, just over the cleft, is a small projection called the "frog stay," since it fits into the plantar cushion and steadies the frog. When the horse's feet are unshod the frog, sole, bars, and bearing edge of the wall are nearly on a level, so that the lower side of the hoof is nearly flat.

The outer horny portions of the hoof, composing everything except the white inner layer, are fibrous in structure, or tubes which run downward in a direction parallel with the general direction of the hoof as a whole. The tubes forming the sole are smaller than those in the wall, and those in the frog are smaller still; but for all that, they are distinctly tubular in form.

There are two kinds of horn, soft horn as composing the outer layer of the wall, the white inner layer, and the frog; the rest of the hoof is composed of hard horn. The soft horn easily absorbs water, and quickly dries out again, and grows brittle and cracks. In quality good horn is fine and tough, bad horn coarse and crumbling, often hard and brittle. All horn is a poor conductor of heat, a most important provision, since it serves to protect the horse's feet alike in very hot countries and in very cold.

The Skin. The skin of the horse consists of three layers, the epidermis, a hard surface of horn-like cells which protects the true skin; the dermis, or leather skin, and the subcutaneous tissue. The second layer or dermis extends over the entire hoof under the horny wall. The epidermis comes to an end above the horny wall in what is called the *frog band*. This resembles the extension of the skin at the base of the human fingernails, and is a hard band extending around the upper edge of the horny hoof, ending in the fleshy frog. It serves to protect the young horn beneath. It is a fifth to a fourth of an inch wide. From this band is secreted the varnish-like outer layer of the wall.

The Coronary Band. This lies under the frog band but above the sensitive laminae. It consists of a convex band four-fifths of an inch wide extending entirely around the foot from one heel to the other. It is more convex in front than at the back, and at the heels is flattened, and this part is called the bar portion. The coronary band secrets the principal part of the horny wall, namely, the thick middle layer, and forms a cushion for its union with the fleshy tissues.

A similar tissue at the bottom of the foot secrets the horny sole and the frog.

The Sensitive Structures. A scientific student should become familiar with the various tendons, muscles, cartilages, arteries and nerves which go to make up the sensitive hoof, but for the purposes of this book a general description will suffice.

Every horseshoer will have noticed how very sensitive the quick of a horse's foot is, and how profusely it bleeds if cut, The outer tissue (the middle skin described above) extends in the general direction of the foot in the form of fleshy leaves, not unlike the leaves of a book, which lie between corresponding horny leaves, each one having a horny leaf on either side. This sensitive structure is a perfect network

of blood--vessels and nerves, and the horse is
thus enabled to feel the slightest pressure or
touch on the outer horny covering. In disease
this sensitiveness causes a great deal of trouble.

In Fig. 11 we see the lines of the extensor
tendon, or front sinew, and the perforans tendon or back sinew, both attached to the coffin
bone. These work over cartilages, and the
perforans tendon works over the navicular bone
above the large cushion which the sensitive
frog forms.

In a thin-skinned, well bred horse the tendons
can be distinctly felt through the skin, and it
is even possible to see their outlines. Frequently, however, these tendons become thickened
from inflammation due to injury, and so they
shorten and draw back the hoof, making the
stubbby-toed animal. When the tendons are
not distended by inflammation and the sinews
and bones are free from all thickenings, we say
the horse has a *clean* leg.

CHAPTER II.

GROWTH AND CONDITION OF THE HOOF.

Growth of the Hoof. Like all parts of living bodies, the hoof continually changes. The horn grows like a fingernail, and unless it is worn off at the bottom or bearing edge, it becomes too long; and if worn off too much, the sensitive portions of the foot do not have sufficient protection and the horse goes lame.

Moreover, when one portion grows unduly it is at the expense of some other. If the heels are too high, the frog diminishes until it is insignificant. In a state of nature, however, the horse's hoof keeps itself perfectly proportioned. If the ground is hard, the horny portion is worn away as fast as it grows; and if the ground is soft, though the horny portion is sometimes overgrown, it soon cracks and breaks away. On cultivated ground, however, a horse must have a very large range indeed if its feet are to be left to take care of themselves. When turned out in the ordinary enclosed pastures, the horse should be brought in periodically to have its feet examined and the growth of horn adjusted.

All shod hoofs become overgrown in from four to five weeks. In such cases there appears to be an access of horn at the toe, since the horny fibres do not grow straight down but obliquely forward. Thus the plantar surface of the foot is carried forward and is thrown out of the proper relation with the rest of the foot, injuriously affecting every part of the foot and indeed the whole leg.

The rate of growth of the wall varies greatly in different horses, and under different surrounding conditions. On an average the wall will grow an inch in three months, and the whole hoof is replaced in from ten to fifteen months. The more actively a horse is exercised, the faster does the hoof grow. Inflammation checks growth, and the effects of it may frequently be seen in rings on the hoof. These rings in themselves are no detriment, but they show possible lameness or illness.

When a hoof is shod, the bearing affects the growth. If there is no bearing on a certain part, it will grow more quickly, and so become even with the portions on which there is bearing. So if the hoof has been broken at the heels or rasped away too much, or for the purpose of removing pressure on any given spot, in a month's time that part will be found, in all probability, to be flush with the shoe.

The only way in which the growth of the horn can be stimulated is by application to the coronary band, as by a mild blister. No ointments applied to the wall will affect the growth, though they may soften the horn a little.

The sole grows in the same way as the wall, but it wears away quite differently. It never becomes overgrown like the wall, for when overgrown it has a tendency to become detached in flakes due to dryness and brittleness. The ordinary movements of the horse cause the dry portions to break up and fall off.

When the frog comes in contact with the ground, it comes off in shreds. If it does not touch the ground, it dries up and sometimes sheds a large outer layer. Though the horn of the frog is softer than that of the wall or the sole, it stands wear as well as either of the other parts, since it is so elastic and rests upon a still more elastic cushion. Under any great pressure, therefore, it yields, and leaves the wall and sole to bear the strain. The growth of the frog depends largely upon the condition of the bars. If they are overgrown, the frog is removed from bearing, and wastes away. High heels are always accompanied by a small frog, and low heels have a large frog.

Horn is porous and absorbs water readily. If too much water is absorbed, the horn is, of course, weakened. The natural protection to this is the varnish-like outer wall, and when this is removed by rasping, moisture is more easily absorbed until the horn beneath beomes hard and dry from exposure and friction. As we have already said, horn is a poor conductor of heat, and therefore if the horn is thick, fitting a hot shoe for a reasonably short time does no harm; but if the horn is thin, fitting a hot shoe must be done quickly or the soft tissue beneath may be damaged.

Although there is always a tendency on the part of nature to correct errors, errors invariably have their penalty. It is very important in shoeing a horse that the bearing surface of the foot on which the shoe is placed is perfectly even and that the horn is equally high on both sides, If one side is trimmed off more than another, in time the side of the wall left too high will become bent, and a crooked hoof results, in which the rings are placed nearer together on the low or concave side than on the high or convex side. So, too, the toe, if left too long, will in time become bent; and heels which are left too long will in two or three months contract just under the coronary band, or curl inward at their lower borders.

Wear of the hoof Affected by Position of Legs. As there are badly formed bodies, so

Fig. 14

there are badly formed hoofs. The form of the hoof depends largely upon the condition of the limb. A straight limb has, as a rule, a well-balanced, regular hoof, while a crooked limb has a hoof to match. Some consideration of limbs is therefore necessary to a true understanding of the wear of hoofs.

To judge the standing position of the fore limbs, one must stand squarely in front of a horse, and for hind limbs squarely behind; or for backward and forward deviations, stand at right angles at the side.   Usually a horse moves according to the way in which he stands, but not always, and the moving position of the horse should also be observed.

If viewed from the front, the limbs when standing should appear perfectly perpendicular

Fig. 15

and a plumb line dropped from the shoulder should pass down the middle of the limb, dividing it equally, and meet the ground at the centre of the toe.

In Figs. 15, 16 and 17 we see various abnormal positions. In Fig. 15 is represented the base-

wide position of the legs, in which the plumb-
line would fall inside the limb and entirely
inside the position of the hoof. A variation of

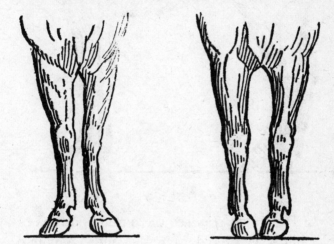

Fig. 16   *Fig. 17*

the same position is shown in **Fig. 16,** where
the knees are knocked in. **Fig. 17** shows the
in-toe position of the feet, a condition in which
the plumb line would fall entirely outside the
hoofs.

The in-toe or base-narrow position is to be
observed not infrequently in horses with wide
breasts. In the bandy-legged position we see
the same narrow base, but the knees are wide
apart.

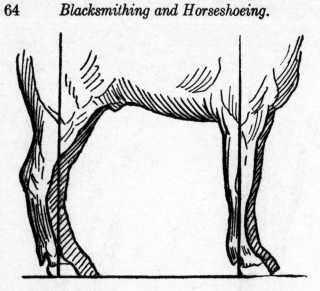

Fig. 18

In Fig. 18 we may see the normal position of the limbs as viewed from the side. A plumb line dropped from the middle of the shoulder blade divides the foreleg into equal parts above the fetlock, and touches the ground just back of the heels. The line formed by the three phalanges of the foot should form an angle of forty-five to fifty degrees with the ground.

In Fig. 19 we see an illustration of the leg that stands too far forward. In Fig. 20 we have the sheep-kneed position, in which the foot stands in about its normal position, but the knee is knocked back and the perpendicular line does not divide the leg in half. In Fig. 21 we see the effect of a weak knee, which allows the foot to rest at too small an angle with the ground, since it is placed too far in front though the limb to the fetlock retains its proper position.

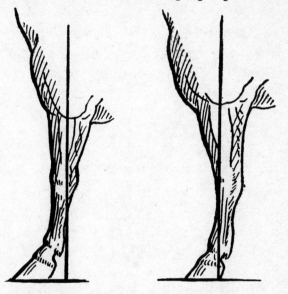

Fig. 19   *Fig. 20*

Similar deviations of the fore foot backward are also frequent; and corresponding to the sheep-kneed position we have the goat-kneed, in which a bulging knee throws the entire hoof behind the perpendicular.

A hind leg is said to be normal when a perpendicular dropped from the bony protuberance of the hip passes through the foot half way between the point of the toe and the heel. The hind limbs as viewed from behind may be base-wide and base-narrow, and even cow-hocked in position, corresponding to the knock-kneed position of the fore limbs, and at the side the foot may be seen to stand considerably back or forward of the perpendicular dropped from the hip joint.

Fig. 21

It is even possible that each limb of the same horse may assume different positions. For instance, the fore-limbs may be base-wide, and the back base-narrow, or the reverse.

In all positions of the limbs we will find the feet assuming one of three forms very nearly. By knowledge of these three forms it is possible to judge the flight of the foot in traveling, and accordingly the preparation of the shoe. These three forms are the *normal*, the *base-wide*, and the *base-narrow*. By the hoof axis (that is, an imaginary line running from the fetlock joint in the general direction of the foot), we may judge the angle at which the hoof meets the ground. In the normal position of the foot the axis of the foot runs straight down and forward at an angle of about forty-five degrees. In the base-wide position it runs obliquely downward and outward, and in the base-narrow it runs obliquely inward. We also have the acute-angled and the obtuse-angled bearing of the hoof. Moreover, the bones below the fet- lock and the wall of the hoof should have exactly the same slant. In the so-called "bear-foot" position, the wall of the hoof runs downward at a much more obtuse angle than the pastern bones (Fig. 22).

If we observe a horse moving freely over level ground, we may see the difference in the carriage of the feet corresponding to the posi- tion of the limbs. When the limbs are normal throughout, the flight of the hoofs is along a

Fig. 22

perfectly straight line, as represented in the
first diagram in Fig. 23.   The toes point straight
forward, and the hoofs alight flat on the ground.

When the limbs stand in the base-wide position, the flight of the hoofs is on the arc of a
circle bowing inward, and the hoof touches
the ground chiefly upon the outer toe.   The
toes may point directly forward, or outward
as in the out-toe position.

The flight of the hoofs from the base-narrow
standing position is just the reverse, namely
in the arc of a circle bowing outward.

There are many variations due to different
conditions.   For instance, a horse pulling a
heavy load, carrying its feet irregularly touches
the ground with the toe first.   Irregular carriage of the feet is not a serious objection to a
horse unless it result in interference or disease
of the joints.

The hoof of the normal position and straight-forward flight has the inner and the outer wall about the same, though the outer may be a little thicker, and somewhat more slanting, describing a slightly larger circle. The height of the wall at the heels, the side, and the toe should be nearly in the proportion of 1:2:3.

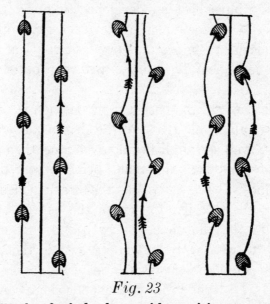

Fig. 23

The hoof of the base-wide position is always irregular, the outer wall being longer and decidedly more slanting than the inner. The bearing edge of the outer wall describes a circle considerably larger, with the sharpest curvature near the heels. If the foot is healthy the frog should be equally developed.   As the irregularity of the hoof is due to the position of the limbs, we should regard it as a normally irregular hoof, to distinguish it from one irregular from disease.

The out-toe position of the feet is marked by a curvature of the outer toe of the bearing-edge, and an inner heel less developed than the inner toe.   The inner toe and outer heel, lying opposite each other, are much less sharply curved. The feet meet the ground with the outer toe first.

The hoof of the base-narrow position is never so irregular as that of the base-wide.   The inner wall is but little more oblique than the outer, the most difference being observed at the heels.   The curve of the bearing-edge of the wall is similar to that of the normal hoof, except that the inner side wall and heel are a little more sharply curved.   Now and then the outer heel is somewhat drawn in under the foot. The form is most pronounced in bandy-legged animals.

The hind hoof is affected in much the same way as the fore hoof.   It is, however, more oval or pointed at the toe, while the fore hoof is round, and it has a very concave sole and a steeper toe.   The angle of the toe with the ground in a hind hoof should be from fifty to fifty-five degrees.

How to Judge a Hoof. Suppose we have a hoof before us and wish to judge it. First we should determine whether it is perfectly healthy or not. A really healthy hoof is not easy to find; but we may recognize a healthy hoof by the following signs:

Looked at as it rests on the ground, either from the front or the side, the course of the wall from the coronet to the ground should be perfectly straight, bent neither in nor out. A straight edge may be placed on the wall, and it should touch at every point. There should be no cracks either up and down or crosswise.

Rings which pass regularly around the hoof parallel to the coronet show nothing more than a little irregularity in the nutrition of the hoof; but if the rings are irregular in any way, even if they are simply more marked at one point than another, though they are parallel to the coronet all the way around, the hoof cannot pass for sound. Marked rings on the hoof of a horse that is well and regularly fed and properly cared for show a weak hoof.

Viewed from the lower side, the bulbs of the

heels should be well rounded and well developed, and in no way displaced.

There should be no separation of the sole along the white line.

The frog should be strong and well developed, equal on both sides, and showing a broad, shallow, dry cleft.

The bars should pass straight inward toward the point of the frog. Any bending outward toward the branches of the sole indicate a narrowing of the space belonging to the frog, or a contraction of the heels.

There should be no red staining of the branches of the sole at the heels. The cartilages above the heels should be elastic, and no part of the hoof should be weakened at the expense of any other portion.

Never judge the form or condition of a hoof without also observing the entire limb.

In order to maintain the hoof in a healthy condition, abundant exercise is indispensable.

CHAPTER III.

SHOEING HEALTHY HOOFS.

The Preliminary Examination. The animal should be examined first at rest and later while in motion. The object is to get an accurate knowledge of the peculiarities of the movements of the limbs, and of the general form and character of the feet and hoofs. It is important to know how the hoof touches and leaves the ground, and the general shape and wear of the shoe, the distribution of nails, etc. At the next shoeing further observations may be made, the original ones being kept in mind, and errors may be corrected.

In examining a horse, first let it be led on a straight line from the observer. The ground over which it passes should be as level as possible. Then have it led back toward the observer, that he may see how the limbs move and how the feet are set on the ground. A few steps taken at a trot will show if the horse is lame, and will also remove any doubt that may exist as to the general and predominating position of the legs. The general object is to determine whether the movements and position of the feet are normal and regular. If they are not, they may be classed as base-wide or base-narrow.

When this matter has been settled, the observer places himself in front and first of all fixes clearly in mind the direction of the foot-axis and notes the general character of the fore hoofs. It is particularly desirable to note if the wall of the hoof has the same slant as the pastern bones, or the leg from the fetlock to the hoof, and whether the wall from the coronet to the bearing-edge is perfectly straight. If there is a curve from top to bottom, it is certain that some part of the wall is unnaturally high, and the base of support is in some way displaced.

In order to gain a complete knowledge of the lines of flight of the hoofs and the positions of the limbs, the horse must be led back and forth a considerable number of times, and this is the more necessary when the standing position is not in every respect normal and the hoofs are different.

Next examine the position of the limbs and the shape of the feet in profile, or from the side. A glance at the whole body will give an idea of the animal's weight, height and length. Then turn to the limbs and hoofs. Especially take note if the form of the hoof corresponds to the position of the limb; then, whether the slant of the fetlock is the same as the wall of the toe, or if the axis of the foot is straight or broken. Also note if the toe is parallel with the heels, for sometimes the toe is bulging and sometimes hollowed out between the coronet and bearing-edge, and the lower edges of the heels may be drawn under the foot.

If there are rings on the wall, their position should be carefully noted. If they cross in any way, thrush of the frog is indicated. At the same time note particularly the length of the shoes.

Next, raise the feet and notice the width of the hoof, the arch of the sole, and the character of the frog. Observe the position of the bulbs of the heels, and see if there are any cracks in the wall. Then look at the old shoes, noting their form, age, position of nailholes and the direction they take, and the general wear the shoes have had. Particularly note if the old shoe corresponds to the form of the hoof, if it entirely covers the wall of the hoof, and if it extends beyond the hoof and in any way has caused interference or irregular wear.

In examining the wear of the shoe, particularly note unusual wear on one side, indicating an irregular way of setting down the foot. If the wear is uneven, an unnatural extension or form of the wall is almost always found, too, especially when the uneven wear has continued for some time. In most cases of that sort it will be found that the worn branch of the shoe is too near the centre of the foot, and the other branch too far. Besides, increased wear indicates that the portion of the wall above it is too high, or that the wall on the opposite side is too low. The twisting movement of many hind feet, for obvious physiological reasons, should not be hindered in the shoeing.

Raising and Holding the Foot. It is well to observe the following directions in raising a foot, though usually no trouble will be experienced if the horse has been accustomed to it.

Never take hold of a foot suddenly or with both hands. See that the horse is standing so that he can easily bear his weight on three legs, and in raising the foot prepare the horse for the act. If the horse does not take a suitable position, move him about a little till his feet are well under his body.

For instance, in raising the left fore foot, stand on the left side facing the animal, speak gently to him, place the right hand on the animal's shoulder, and with the left rub down the limb *at the front.* Gently press the horse over toward the right side, and as soon as the weight has been shifted on to the other side, the animal naturally lifts his foot from the ground. Now grasp the foot from the inside below the fetlock with the right hand, following with the left upon the outside, turn partly to the right, and support the horse's foot upon the left leg, standing as quietly and firmly as possible. Never hold the foot higher than the elbow joint, and usually somewhat lower.

In lifting the left hind foot, stroke the animal back to the hip with the left hand, supporting the hand upon it while the right strokes the limb downward, grasping it behind. Press the animal over toward the right side with the left hand, and with the right hand loosen the foot and carry it forward and outward so that it is bent at the hock. Then turn your body toward the right and bring the left leg against the outer side of the fetlock joint, carry the foot backward, and pass the left arm over the croup to the inner side of the hock. Finally the pastern is held in both hands.

Be careful in lifting a foot not to pinch or squeeze a foot or lift it so high as to give unneces-

sary pain. Work quietly, rapidly, causing
as little pain as possible, and the results will
be correspondingly more satisfactory. Especially be careful not to lift the foot of a young
horse too high, and from time to time let the
foot down to rest. Also in the case of
old and stiff horses, beware of lifting the feet
too high, especially when beginning work.

Vicious horses must be handled severely in
many cases. Watch the ears and eyes, and
immediately punish any symptom of temper.
This may be done by loud words or by jerking
the halter. If this does not do any good, make
the horse back rapidly over a piece of soft
ground till he is tired out.

To help in supporting the hind foot, a leather
band or plaited rope may be fastened into the
tail and passed around the foot below the fetlock, the lower end being held by the hand.
This compels the horse to support a part of
the weight of the limb, and prevents damage
from kicking. Before placing this band around
the fetlock, the front foot on the same side
should be raised.

Before casting a refractory horse or placing
it in stocks, an experienced man should hold it
by the bridle and attempt to soothe it by gentle
words and caresses till he gains its confidence.

Ticklish horses must be taken hold of firmly, for light touches are to such animals more unpleasant than rougher handling. In the case of many ticklish horses, the feet may be raised if taken hold of suddenly without any preparatory movements.

Taking Off the Old Shoes. If a horse's hoofs are healthy, all the old shoes may be taken off at the same time; but there are cases in which this is not advisable.

In taking off the shoe, do not wrench it violently, but draw it off cautiously and slowly. Dirty hoofs should first be cleaned with a stiff brush. Lift the clinch with a rather dull clinch-cutter, and take pains not to injure the horn of the wall. Next, lift the entire shoe slightly, either with broad-billed pincers, or by driving the nail-cutter between the shoe and the hoof. In the first case the branches of a shoe should be well circled, and the pincers moved only in the direction of the branches.

Much twisting of the hoof is liable to strain the ligaments, and to guard against this the hoof should be supported with the left hand or with the leg just above the knee.

Preparing the Hoof for Shoes. The preparation of the hoof for the shoe, usually spoken of as paring or trimming, is a most important matter. Its object is to shorten the hoof, which has grown too long under the shoe. The tools needed are the rasp and the hoof-knife. On large or hard hoofs a pair of sharp nippers or a sharp hewing knife with flat, smooth sides may be used to hasten the work.

The hoof is first cleansed and the stubs of old nails are removed. Bearing in mind the examination of the hoof and limb previously made ask yourself how much horn is to be removed and just where. In any case, remove loose or detached portions of the wall, and scrape off the flakes of dead horn from the sole. Then run the rasp around the wall and break it off to the depth to which it should be shortened.

Rule. Cut the wall down to the sole so that not less than one-tenth of an inch of the surface of the sole comes into the level of the bottom edge of the wall.

The whole bearing surface, including the edge of the sole and the white line, may be rasped until horizontal. The point of the toe may be turned up a little, however.

In dressing the frog, always leave it so that it will project beyond the bearing surface about the thickness of a flat shoe. Do not weaken it by paring, else it will lose its activity and shrink, and the hoof will become narrow.

Never trim the frog at all unless it is too prominent, except to remove loose or diseased portions when the frog is affected by thrush.

Never shorten the bars except when too long. In no case weaken their union with the sole. They should be left nearly as high as the walls at the heels, and the branches of the sole should lie about a twelfth of an inch lower.

The angles of the bars with the wall require attention. In unshod hoofs the bars run straight back, but in shod hoofs the buttresses (as the angles are called) curl inward and press upon the frog, causing it to shrink. In such cases the elongated pieces of horn should be removed so as to make the bars straight.

Rule. The sharp edge of the lower side of the wall should be rasped until the bearing surface of the wall is no wider than the actual thickness of the wall along a line perpendicular to the outer face.

In healthy hoofs, however, when the wall is straight from the coronet to the bearing surface, the varnish-like outer surface should never be rasped much above the bearing-edge. The only exception is when there is an outward bending of the lower edge of the wall, usually on the inner side wall and heel.

In regard to the inclination of the plantar

plane to the foot axis, note that in the regular
position of the limbs, the inner and outer walls
should be of about the same height; in the base-
wide position, the outer wall is higher than the
inner, and in the base-narrow position, the inner wall is higher. Observation from the side
will show the relative elevation of the toe in
regard to the heels. The wall of the hoof and
the long pastern should have the same slope.
If, however, the hoof has become too long under
the shoe, the axis of the foot will be broken at
the coronet and the wall and the long pastern
will not have the same slant.   (See Fig. 24.)

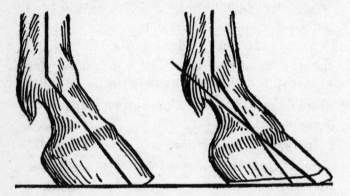

Fig. 24

Rule. The bearing surface of the foot should
be so corrected that as the horse moves it will
be placed flat upon the ground, and the walls

of the hoof, in whatever direction they are
viewed, will be parallel with the axis of the
bones.

Great care must be taken in changing from
flat shoes to those with calks or the reverse,
that the foot be so treated that it will set flat
on the ground when the new shoes are on. Each
foot should be set down on the ground and carefully observed after it has been trimmed before
the new shoe is put on. It should also be
compared carefully with the opposite hoof.
Until such an examination has been made, can
the hoof be said to be properly prepared for
shoeing? Each pair of hoofs (fore and hind)
should not only be equal, but also in proper
proportion to the weight of the body.

Preparing the Hoof for Going Barefoot.
Observe first, that to go barefoot the hoof
must have plenty of horn.

After the shoe has been removed the frog
should be pared down nearly even with the wall,
and the sharp edge of the wall should be rounded
off, in some cases as far as the white line. If
this is not done, large pieces of the wall will
break away. The more slanting the wall, the
more must a hoof be rounded. Going barefoot
strengthens the hoof, but hoofs without shoes
should be examined from time to time and any

growing fault in the shape or direction of the horn corrected without delay. The sharp edge of the wall will in many cases have to be rounded again and again, especially if the walls are very oblique, and the heels may be shortened, since they are not always worn away as rapidly as the toe.

Making Shoes. Besides a good, tough iron, the following tools are required: An anvil with a round horn and a hole at one end, a round-headed hammer, a round sledge, a stamping hammer, a reliable steel pritchel, and a round fuller. The workman must be quick and have a good eye. A shoe should be made with care, yet quickly enough to take advantage of the heat.

To make a flat shoe, find the length of the hoof from the angles of the heels to the toe and the greatest width. These two measurements added together give the length of the bar required. The bar selected should be one which will require the least amount of working. Of course in case heel calks are required, the bar must be proportionately longer.

In making a front shoe (Fig. 25) the bar should be heated to a white heat just beyond the middle. Run over it lightly with the hammer, turn it on edge, work it down a trifle,

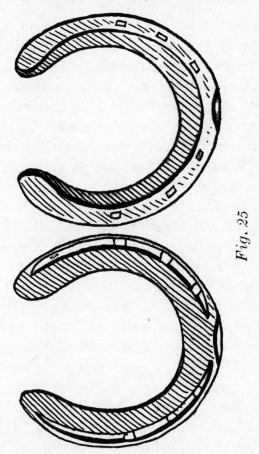

Fig. 25

make a quarter turn to the right and hammer the entire half to a diamond shape. With a half turn to the left, flatten the right edge to within three quarters of an inch of the end, hammer smooth, turn the ground face up and gently bend the branch. Holding the branch by the outer edge, bend it into a semicircle with the round head of the hammer. The sledge may be used in concaving it, which should be done immediately. The concaving should terminate three-fourths of an inch from the end.

Next fuller the branch, setting the fuller about a twelfth of an inch from the edge for small shoes, a little more for large shoes, and proceeding toward the toe. Do this twice to make the fullering deep enough. Next stamp the holes and punch them through with the pritchel, run over the surfaces and edges, finishing the outer edge upon the horn, and finally hammer the bearing side perfectly smooth and horizontal. Treat the left branch the same, but carry the fullering from the toe to the heel. An ordinary shoe should be completed in two heats, and a pair of shoes in from eight to fifteen minutes.

The hind shoe is made like the front shoe, except that it is curved as shown in Fig. 26, and concaving is unnecessary, though the inner edge of the hoof surface should be rounded. As the inner side of the shoe is thickened in bending in proportion as the outer edge is stretched, care must be taken to even the side up by hammering the shoe smooth.

The Character of a Shoe. Every peculiarity

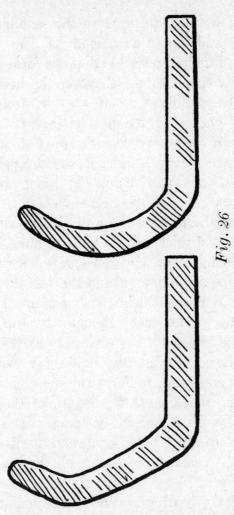

Fig. 26

of the hoof or the position of the limbs and manner of wear requires a corresponding shoe. The
character of the shoe is of the utmost impor-

tance if we wish to preserve the soundness of the feet and legs of an animal.

First, it is indispensable that the form of the shoe correspond to the shape of the hoof. It should be possible at a glance to tell a front and a hind shoe, a right and a left apart. *Front shoes must be round at the toe; hind shoes must be pointed at the toe,* though not too much pointed.

Second, all shoes should be wider webbed at the toe than at the heels, averaging about twice the thickness of the wall of the hoof.

Third, the thickness of the shoe must correspond to the wear, and must be thick enough not to require renewing under a month. The average required thickness is perhaps seven-sixteenths of an inch, though the thickness should be lessened if the wear is to be less than the average. Ordinarily, all shoes without calks should be of uniform thickness.

Fourth, in all cases the length of the shoe should be great enough to cover the entire bearing-surface of the hoof, and in draught horses the branches should reach the bulbs of the heels.

Fifth, the bearing portion of the upper side of the shoe should be wide enough to cover the wall, the white line, and from a twelfth to an eighth of an inch of the margin of the sole.

The concaving is intended to prevent interference with the concave portion of the sole, and if the sole is very concave so that there is no danger of its touching the shoe, concaving of the shoe is not necessary. The ground side of the shoe should be perfectly smooth and horizontal, except for the rolling up of the toe.

Sixth, the outer edge of the shoe should slope gently under the hoof, so that the ground surface will be smaller than the hoof surface. This tends to prevent interfering, or loosening of the shoe from knocking against outside objects. The inner border should be slightly rounded.

Seventh, the depth of the fullering should be about two-thirds of the thickness of the shoe, uniform in width, and clean. The object of it is to make the shoe lighter in proportion to its size. Besides, it aids in making the nailholes uniform, and gives the shoe a rougher ground surface.

Eighth, the nailholes have an importance that can hardly be overstated, for upon their character, distribution, etc., depends the stability of the shoe, as well as the avoidance of injuring the sensitive foot, or splitting or breaking the horn, and interference with the elasticity of the foot.

A proper nailhole should taper evenly from

the ground surface to the hoof surface, like a tunnel. For a medium shoe, six nailholes should be sufficient; but for a heavy shoe, especially one with heel and toe calks, eight holes are required. In the latter case it is not absolutely necessary that every nailhole should contain a nail. Hind shoes usually require one more nailhole than front shoes, though seldom more than eight. In front shoes the nailholes may extend back to the middle of each branch, while in hind shoes they may extend two-thirds of the way back; but nails should never be put in the toes. The distance of the nailholes from the outer border will depend upon the thickness of the wall of the hoof, and should be equal to the perpendicular thickness of the wall (not the slanting thickness on the ground surface of the hoof). It is clear, therefore, that the distance of the nailholes from the border will vary as the thickness of the wall of the hoof varies.

The direction of the nailholes must correspond to the slant of the wall. Nailholes near the toes should usually incline somewhat inward, those on the sides should incline less, and those toward the heels should be perpendicular to the bearing surface of the shoe.

Ninth, clips are the small ears drawn upward

from the outer edge of the shoe. All shoes should have clips at the toes, and a side clip should be drawn up on that side of a shoe which first meets the ground as the animal moves. The clips prevent shifting or slipping of the shoe, and should be higher and thicker on the hind than on the front shoes. They should be about as high (on a flat shoe) as the thickness of the shoe, while on shoes with calks they should be somewhat higher. They should be strong and without flaw where they leave the shoe.

Heel Calks. All calks on normal hoofs should be so adjusted as to interfere as little as possible with the setting down of the foot, and so that the wear will be uniform. The branches, therefore, should be a little thinner just in front

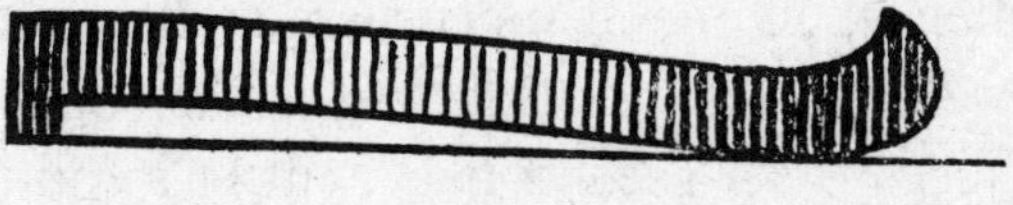

Fig. 27

of the calks than is the toe. A front shoe with heel calks must be comparatively long, and should be rolled considerably at the toe, the upward turn beginning at the inner border. Heel calks may be three or four cornered and somewhat conical, and should not be higher than the thickness of the shoe. The branches should not rise excessively, but assume about the direction shown in Fig. 27.

Toe and Heel calks. If there are to be both toe and heel calks, the thickness of the shoe should be uniform, and the calks should be somewhat longer than if there are to be only heel calks.

The toe calks should never be higher than the heel calks.

Toe calks are formed by welding a piece of steel to the toe. They may be of three kinds:

1 *Sharp Toe Calks.* One corner of a rather wide piece of toe steel is drawn to a sharp point, and when the shoe has been heated to a white heat this sharp point is driven into the middle of the toe. At the first heat, this piece of steel standing upon one of its corners is driven down and welded from the centre to the right and left corners. A second heat will be required to complete the work.

2 *Blunt Toe Calk.* This is a somewhat long, four-cornered piece of steel with an ear on one edge. It is welded on in one heat.

3 *Coffin-Lid Toe Calk.* This is like the blunt calk, but the side that is to be welded to the shoe is broader and longer than the ground side.

They may be put on at one heat. This kind
can be more securely welded to the shoe and is
suitable for winter, as is the first kind.

Calks injure the elasticity of the foot and the
joints, since they raise the frog off the ground,
and furnish a smaller base of support than a
flat shoe. They are, nevertheless, indispensable
on slippery roads, especially in winter. When
conditions will permit they should be dispensed
with, especially on the front feet.

*Peculiarities of shoes for Different Kinds of
Hoofs.* 1. *Shoe for a Normal Hoof.* For a
normal foot a shoe should be moderately bevelled under the foot all around, and should be
longer than the hoof by about the thickness of
the shoe.

2. *Shoe for a very Sloping or Acute-Angled
Hoof.* Such a shoe should be strongly bevelled
under near the toe on the outer edge, but gradually becoming perpendicular near the ends of
the branches. The nailholes at the toe should
incline inward somewhat more than usual, but
otherwise should be regular. The length should
be somewhat greater than in the case of a shoe
for the normal hoof.

3. *Shoe for Bear-Shaped or Stumpy Hoof.*
The outer edge should be perpendicular at the
toe, or even bevelled slightly outward if the

hoof is very upright. The last nail should be placed just beyond the middle of the shoe. The shoe should be short, not over a tenth of an inch longer than the hoof. In the case of a hoof not only stumpy but "bear-foot," the shoe should be long, however.

4. *Shoe for Base-wide Hoof.* The outer branch should have the outer edge bevelled inward, the inner branch nearly perpendicular. The holes in the outer branch of the shoe should extend well back, while on the inner branch they are to be crowded forward toward the toe. The length will depend upon the slope of the foot, the more sloping hoof requiring the longer shoe.

5. *Shoe for Base-narrow Hoof.* The outer edge of the outer branch should be bevelled outward, the inner branch should be bevelled strongly inward. The nailholes in the outer branch should be crowded toward the toe, and on acount of the greater width of this branch, may be punched farther in than the wall is thick. On the inner branch, the nailholes are to be distributed farther back and punched light. The length will depend upon the slant of the hoof. The outer branch should be an eighth of an inch longer than the inner.

On a wide hoof the web of the shoe should be

wider than usual, and bevelled under the hoof all around, while the nailholes should be carried well back. On a narrow hoof the outer edge should be bevelled somewhat under the toe, but should be nearly perpendicular elsewhere, and the nailholes distributed as usual but nearly perpendicular, inclining somewhat outward near the heels, and near the toe inclining somewhat inward. On narrow hoofs concaving is usually unnecessary.

The Choice of the Shoe. This is not at all difficult after we have taken into account the weight, kind of work, standing position, gait, form of hoofs, and quality of horn. We usually choose a shoe longer than the hoof, because in growing the hoof carries the shoe forward with it, and because the heels gradually wear away by rubbing and become lower. For heavy hauling, shoes with toe and heel calks should extend back to support the bulbs of the heels; but trotting or riding horses require shorter shoes.

In deciding the weight of the shoe, consider whether the legs are used up by work or not, and the general character of the work for which the horse is used. The shoes should also be heavy enough to wear a month. Hard roads and a heavy gait require strong, durable shoes, and in some cases they may be made durable by welding in steel. For light work and soft roads, use light shoes. Running horses require very thin, narrow shoes made of steel.

Fitting Shoes. The circumference of the hoof side of a shoe should always correspond exactly to the circumference of the hoof itself when dressed, and should fit the bearing-side of the hoof air tight. All defects in the surface of the hoof and the shoe, and in the nailholes, must be carefully remedied during the fitting process. A perfectly horizontal bearing surface is very important, especially at the heels, and the bearing surface should be quite smooth. Entirely uniform heating is absolutely necessary in shaping shoes, because with an irregular heat the shoe is likely to get twisted at the warm spots. The shoe should be perfectly straight, and should be held up before the eye edgewise to see that one side just covers the view of the other. Flat shoes should be laid upon a level surface to see that they touch at every point, except at the rolling toe.

Front shoes should be slightly rolled up at the toe. In most cases the roll should begin about the middle of the web, and should extend up about half the thickness of the iron. The roll ensures a uniform wear of the shoe.

The shoe, fairly hot, should be placed on the foot so that the toe clip will come directly in front of the point of the frog, and the scorched horn should be repeatedly removed with the rasp until a perfect-fitting bed for the shoe has been made. The horn sole should not be burnt, because the velvety tissue of the sole lies directly above it. *The nailholes must under all circumstances cover the white line.*

The shoes should correspond with the outer edge of the wall of the hoof near the nailholes, but farther back toward the heels the shoe should widen until at the extremities it is a twenty-fifth to a twelfth of an inch beyond the hoof. This makes the shoes wear longer. In hind shoes, however, the inner branch should closely follow the wall, to prevent interfering and loosening the shoe with the other foot.

Between the ends of the branches and the frog there should be room enough to pass a toothpick.

Important Rule. If the form of the hoof is natural, and has not been altered by artificial treatment, the shoe should in every case have the form of the hoof; but if the hoof has been changed, we should try to give the shoe the form that the hoof had before the change took place. Such treatment cannot injure the hoof, and in time it will bring the hoof back to its original form.

In a regular foot we have seen that the shoe should fit the foot, the nailholes come directly over the white line, and there should be a little space between the frog and the branches.

In irregularly shaped hoofs we must consider not only the form of the hoof, but the position of the limbs and the distribution of bearing. *Where the most weight falls the supporting surface must be broader, and where the least weight falls, the bearing surface should be narrower.* Thus the irregular distribution of weight in an abnormal hoof is regulated. The way in which this is done in the various kinds of hoofs is as follows:

In an acute-angled hoof the shoes must be long, because most of the weight comes at the back, while the toe may be made narrow by turning in or bevelling under.

In an obtuse-angled hoof the conditions are reversed, and the surface of support should be increased at the toe and lessened toward the heels, the nailholes being directed straight or slightly outward.

A base-wide hoof requires most support upon the inner side, which should be widened while the outer side is narrowed.

The base-narrow hoof requires just the reverse.

In the normal foot the ends of the branches should be equally distant from the cleft of the frog; but this is not the case in base-wide and base-narrow hoofs. In the base-wide the outer and in the base-narrow the inner branch should be farther from the cleft.

The wide hoof has too large a base of support, and so should be narrowed by bevelling the shoe under.

The narrow hoof has too small a base of support, and it must not be made smaller, and the outer border should be perpendicular.

Shoeing Heavy Draught Horses. If the hoofs have become injured or distorted, shoes in the case of heavy draught horses must be slightly modified. The following points should especially be noted. Every one of them is important.

If the hoof is out of shape, the shoe must be so set as to come directly beneath every point of the coronet, even if it projects somewhat beyond the wall at the heels. The opposite branch may usually follow the wall closely.

The new should be made fuller and wider where the old shoe shows most wear.

Especially remember, the shoe should be set farther toward the most worn side. This renders unnecessary the common practice of bending out the outer branch and heel calks of hind shoes.

Concluding Directions as to Fitting. When the shoer is satisfied with the fit of the shoe, it should be cooled, and brightened with a file, and the nailholes opened with an oiled pritchel. All sharp edges should be carefully filed down. In filing the outer border, file lengthwise, not crosswise. Care must be taken not to bend the shoe by improperly clamping it in the vise.

Nailing the Shoe. This is the process of fastening the shoes on by special nails known as horseshoe nails.

The nails whether made by hand or machine should be of the best wrought iron, slender, wedge-shaped, and twice as wide as they are thick. The thickness must correspond to the length. Never should the nail be longer than is absolutely necessary in fastening the shoe. Six to nine sizes are required.

The rough nails must go through a process of shaping and bevelling to prepare them for the hoof. While being made smooth and even they *should be hammered as lightly as possible.*

The nails must also be so shaped that they will go through the horn straight and not curved. A perfectly straight nail will pass through the horn in a curve, and not only does not hold well, but is liable to injure the sensitive tissues. *Therefore curve the nail a little* so that the concave side will be toward the frog.

The nail is to be bevelled at the point so that it will form a one-sided wedge, with the slanting side on the inside (Fig. 28). Nails driven low

Fig. 28

should have a short bevel, nails driven high a longer bevel. Never allow the bevel to form a hook, and make it sharp but not thin, and under no conditions imperfect. Machine-made nails, ready for use, are to be preferred, though hand-made nails are tougher.

Be perfectly certain the shoe is absolutely

perfect in shape and fit before beginning to nail. In nailing the horn should be spared as much as possible, and never should the sensitive tissue be injured.

The nails should always pass through the white lines, and thence straight through the wall, neither too high nor too low. If too high, there is danger of pricking, if too low the nailholes will tear out easily when being clinched.

In driving a nail, hold it in the fingers as long as possible in order to preserve the correct direction. At each stroke of the hammer the nail should penetrate one-fifth to one-fourth of an inch. Hard driving and light tapping should never be permitted.

When at a depth of five-eighths of an inch nails are going soft, bending, giving a dull sound, or causing pain, they should at once be withdrawn.

Nails should be driven from five-eighths to an inch and five-eighths high, according to the size of the horse and the hoof.

As soon as the nail has been driven in, its point should be bent down toward the shoe, to avoid possible injuries. The nails should then be gone over with the hammer till they are driven well down into their holes, the hoof being supported with the left hand. Pincers should then be held under the bent nails and they should be bent still more by sharp blows on the heads of the nails.

Nip off the points near the hoof, the horn that has been broken out by bending the nails down is to be rasped off, and the ends of the nails bent still more, but not quite even with the wall. A clinching block is now placed under the nails and they are clinched still closer to the walls, care being taken not to bend them within the wall. Finally, with the edge of the hammer the nail is driven down flush with the wall.

Of course all the nails should be driven in and turned down before clinching begins.

On the inner wall, the clinches should be so smooth they cannot be felt when the finger is passed over them.

If any horn projects beyond the shoe around the toe, it should be rasped away carefully in the direction in which the wall slants, but never higher than the clinches. Finally, remove the sharp lower edge of the wall by running the rasp around between the shoe and the horn.

A clinch is said to be long enough when it is equal to the width of the nail at the point where it occurs.

A shoeing stool is useful in clinching the nails

on the front hoofs. The hind hoofs can be clinched in the hand.

When the shoeing is finished, the horse should be led out to see if the new shoeing has accomplished the purpose assumed at the start.

Last of all, cover the entire hoof with a thin layer of hoof-salve.

CHAPTER IV.

FORGING AND INTERFERING.

Forging is that peculiarity of gait in a horse by which the toe of the hind foot strikes the branches of the front shoe at the heels. It makes an unpleasant noise, and is dangerous to the horse. It may result in wounding the heels of the fore feet, and damages the toes of the hind, besides often pulling off the front shoes.

The causes for forging may be: 1. because the horse stands higher at the croup than at the withers, or has a short body and long legs, or "stands under" in front or behind (that is, the feet come inside the perpendicular from shoulder or hip joint); or 2. because of unskilful driving over heavy ground, or riding a horse without holding him down at the mouth and by pressing his sides with the knees; or again 3. because of simple fatigue, which may cause interfering even in well built horses; or, finally, 4. because of poor shoeing, such as long toes behind, or shoes in front that are too long.

To correct forging it is necessary to use front shoes that are no longer and no wider than the hoof. The ends of the branches backward should be bevelled down and forward under the foot, even when heel calks are used. If the horse forges upon the lower surface of the branches at the heels, this surface may be concaved. The hind shoes are to be shortened at the toe, and the lower edges at the toe well rounded. In place of a toe clip, substitute two side clips, and so fit the shoe that three-fourths of the thickness of the wall, of course with the edge well rounded, will extend beyond the shoe.

Interfering describes the condition in which one hoof in motion strikes the adjoining leg. It is liable to injure the coronary band, the fetlock, or even the cannon bone as high as the knee, and lameness often results.

The causes of interfering lie either in the shoeing, in the position of the limbs, or the way in which the animal is worked. Well shod horses never interfere when their standing position is correct. Horses that stand base-wide interfere sometimes, and interfering is often found in horses whose legs narrow into the fetlock while their toes turn out. Traces of unequal length, delay in shoeing, and fatigue are also frequent causes.

When a horse is found to interfere, he should first be carefully examined to determine the cause. If it is due to a twisted position of the shoe, hoofs too wide, or raised clinches, the remedy is obvious. If it is due to the position of the limbs, we must first find the exact part of the foot that does the striking. Carefully regulating the bearing surface, the shoe may be made straight along the place where interfering occurs and the hoof narrowed at this point. Also in fitting the shoe, one-third of the thickness of the wall may extend beyond the border of the shoe. In serious cases we **may** use a shoe with no nails in the inner branch.

Fig. 29

Fig. 29 shows the so-called "interfering" shoe, the inner branch of which is higher than the outer, and it is so shaped that the hoof will project somewhat beyond it. It may be recommended for use when the limbs stand base-narrow. Each shoe must be carefully shaped to meet each individual case, and the nailholes on the inner branch should be punched somewhat nearer the edge than usual.

Fig. 30

"The dropped-crease" interfering shoe is shown in Fig. 30. The only nailhole in the inner branch is at the toe. Such a shoe is valuable for a hind hoof on a foot in which the toe turns out, but better results may be obtained by using a shoe whose inner branch is straight and with-

out nails at the striking place. Such a shoe
may be fitted wide at the heels, and the inner
heel calk should be higher than the outer,
while the outer branch should be as narrow as

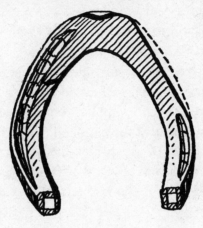

Fig. 31

it can be made (Fig. 31). To prevent shifting
on such a shoe, a side clip should be drawn up
on the outside.

The simpler and lighter the shoe, the less will
horses interfere. No shoeing will prevent interfering in case of fatigue or bad harnessing.

CHAPTER V.

WINTER SHOEING. CARE OF THE HOOF.

What is called *winter shoeing* consists in providing the bearing surface of shoes with some means to prevent slipping on ice and snow. Sharp projections are supplied, and the problem is to keep these projections sharp.   When the ground is well covered with snow, all sharp shoes will remain sharp; and when the ground

Fig. 32

is open and only partially covered with snow, no shoes will remain sharp. No entirely satisfactory method of sharpening has yet been discovered.

Ice-Nails. The simplest method of sharpening is to replace one or two nails on each branch with ice-nails, as shown in Fig. 32. This method of sharpening is also the least durable.

Sharp Calks. These are made by welding a sharp steel wedge into the outer calks when they have been split. The shoe is laid on the edge of the anvil and sharpened from within outward, so that the calk shall be thin from the branch to the ground, and the outer side be in a straight line with the border. If the calk is narrow all the way, a sharp edge is not needed. Never sharpen the inner calk unless the ground is unusually slippery. The inner calk should be sharpened at right angles to the direction of the branch, as shown in Fig. 33, and the outer

Fig. 33

corner rounded.   The calk on the outer branch
is shown in Fig. 34.

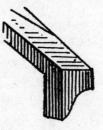

Fig. 34

For heavy draught horses a toe calk is required.   This consists of toe-steel welded firmly
to the shoe.   All calks should be tempered in
order as much as possible to increase their durability.   This may be done by sticking into
moist sand as far as the tap and allowing to
cool slowly from a cherry-red heat.

Screw Calks.   Various machine-made screw
calks may be had, and should always be made
of steel.   Any ordinary shoe may be fitted with
them by making holes in the ends of the branches
with a cylindrical hammer punch and cutting a
thread.   The hole should be moderately counter-
sunk on the lower side, and the shoulder of the
calk should rest in the counter-sinking.   The
thread should be clean and deep, but not too
coarse, and all calks should have the same sized

thread and tap. A tap of one-half inch in diameter is sufficient for the heaviest shoes. Screw toe-calks are liable to become loose. The great advantage of screw heel calks is that they can be changed while the shoe is on the hoof, and blunt or sharp calks may be put on as the work requires. They have a tendency to loosen and break off unless well made and of the best material; but if care is taken they are the best heel calks that can be used. Square and round peg calks are cheaper and more easily made, but are not so satisfactory as screw calks.

Removable heel calks that do not need sharpening have been invented and are to be recommended for city use where horses must often travel upon bare pavements even when the snow lies on the ground. They have sharpened faces of various shapes, such as that of an H or an X. The wider and more extensive the wearing surface presented by the calk the more durable will it prove. Calks with narrow edges and few surfaces presented to the ground become dull most quickly. Such calks are not required in the country.

To Prevent Balling with Snow use shoes with narrow web concave upon the ground surface, and keep the frog and sole well oiled. Sole pads of leather, felt, or straw serve the same end. The best method is to use a rubber sole and frog pad. There is also a patent hoof cement which is to be recommended.

Care of Unshod Hoofs. The care of the hoofs of colts is very important. Abundant exercise on dry ground free from stones is the first requirement. Such exercise will cause the hoofs to wear in a regular manner. Care should be taken, however, to see from time to time if the wear is uniform, and if it is not it should be corrected by the rasp.

If colts are reared in the barn the hoof does not receive sufficient wear and various difficulties are sure to result. The wall becomes too long and sometimes separates from the sole, and the wall bends. Weak heels bend inward upon the frog; the toe becomes much too long, and this affects the pastern, throwing it out of position and spoiling the gait. Therefore hoofs should be shortened from time to time. The heels which curve in should be pared with the hoof-knife, and the outer edge of the bearing wall rounded. Sometimes the hoof must be readjusted in bearing level to prevent distortion, and by this means the position of the limbs may be corrected if bad. If taken in time, a good hoof can be produced.

Washing. It is highly desirable to preserve cleanliness in all stable-reared colts by frequently and thoroughly washing the hoofs and taking care there is a good bedding of straw.

Time to Shoe. Too early shoeing is very injurious, as it interferes with the development of the hoof. When shod too soon, colts are often overworked and thereby ruined. Moderate work in the fields does not harm your horses, but for this shoes are not required.

Hoofs of Older Horses. The unshod hoofs of older horses should be rounded at regular intervals and the length of the walls regulated when proper wear has not taken place.

Care of Shod Hoofs. Though shoeing is absolutely necessary, shod hoofs are more liable to injury than unshod. Shoeing prevents the natural movements of the foot, interferes with circulation, hinders the growth of horn, and finally causes a gradual shrinking of the hoof. Keeping horses in stables is also injurious, since it prevents free movement, is unclean when the floors are bad and the bedding filthy, and causes dryness of the hoof. Continual standing invariaby makes the hoofs contract, and dryness adds to the evil, more especially in the front hoofs. Hind hoofs receive sufficient moisture from the manure. Uneven floors tire the limbs. Accumulation of manure and stationary sole-pads induce thrush of the frog.

With proper care these evils may be lessened or entirely removed. Not only should the hoofs be shortened every four or five weeks, but proper attention should be given to cleanliness and moisture. These require dry straw and daily picking out and washing of the feet. Such measures will prevent thrush in the hind feet, and daily washing will give the front feet the necessary moisture. Washing adds greatly to the elasticity of the shod hoof. To keep the moisture in, the entire hoof should be oiled or coated with hoof-salve. Patent salves are not needed. Melted horse-grease, pork fat, or any other fat that is not rancid will answer.

Abundant (but not excessive) exercise is especially necessary to keep the hoof healthy. By keeping up the circulation of blood it stimulates the growth of horn. Horses which work regularly have better hoofs, as a rule, than those which stand in the stable. A poultice of clay, bran, sawdust, or linseed meal is never necessary if the hoofs have proper care; but there are times when this is useful on front feet. The feet may even be stood in pails of water. Front hoofs are much more subject to dryness

than hind, and the shoe aids in this as it keeps
the foot off the ground. Oiling alone will not
soften horn. It must always be accompanied
by washing in water, and it is the water which
softens. Oiling before a hoof has been cleaned
is decidedly injurious, as it produces a greasy
crust under which the horn becomes brittle.

The surest sign of a clean hoof is the color of
the horn. It will appear translucent even after
it has been covered with ointment. Black-
ened ointments should never be used, as they
prevent properly judging the condition of the
hoof. When the roads are wet and muddy, a
little wax or rosin may be added to the ointment,
as it prevents too great softening of the horn.

As all shoeing, even the best, injures the hoof
more or less, horses should occasionally be allowed to go barefoot, and the more the better.
This applies especially to horses out of service,
provided the nature of the hoof permits going
barefoot.

CHAPTER VI.

Lameness. Usually we do not consider a hoof defective unless there is lameness; but there may be disease, and we must consider that there is whenever the appearance of the hoof deviates from the normal as previously described. Front hoofs are more easily affected than hind hoofs, because they bear greater weight and have more slanting walls. All sound hoofs varying in shape from the normal or regular are more liable to disease when the wall is slanting or distorted than when stumpy or obtuse-angled.

Inflammation of the Pododerm. The Pododerm is the sensitive skin under the horny wall and sole. It shows itself in nearly every case by lameness, and on close examination it will be found that there is increased heat in the hoof, and a stronger pulsation in the arteries, together with pain. The pain gives a timid, shortened gait, especially on hard ground; and sensitiveness may be detected by pressing on the hoof with the pincers, or lightly tapping the hoof. The increased heat may be detected by touch of the hand. Intense pain and great heat between the hoof and the fetlock indicate suppuration.

A lame horse should be systematically examined as previously described in the judging of a horse for shoeing. Usually there will be no doubt whether the lameness is in the hoof or in other joints, but in cases of doubt all the joints and tendons of the foot may be examined.

The old shoe should be removed with the greatest caution. Sometimes the second shoe must not be removed till the first has been replaced. Equal caution should be observed in paring, which may be looked on as a part of the examination. Paring for the shoeing of a lame hoof often differs from paring under normal conditions, but it often leads to exact knowledge of the source of the trouble.

The causes of disease of the hoof are various, but arise from bruising of the tender parts shut up within the horny cover, for the most part. This arises from unskilful dressing of the feet, bad shoeing, overwork in the case of a young horse, too great dryness, etc.

Treatment. First, the cause should be discovered and removed as far as possible. Often lameness may be removed by proper shoeing, change in the work done, and better care of the feet. When the inflammation is intense, the shoe should be removed for a few days. When the inflammation is moderate, and confined to some particular spot, it is sufficient to alter the shoeing so as to regulate the distribution of weight, and removing all superfluous horn, especially from the wall and sole, in order to make the horn more yielding and the poultices more effective. The shoe should then be so fitted that the diseased portion will be relieved of the weight of the body and remain free from all pressure. This can be done partly by making the branch covering the affected portion longer and wider, partly by cutting down the bearing edge of the wall where this can be done without weakening the wall and also by concaving the upper surface of the shoe. As difficulties are more usual in the back part of the hoof, it is advisable to put the nailholes as far front as practicable.

The Bar-Shoe. This form of shoe (shown in Fig. 35) holds the first place among special shoes for lame feet, and in many cases is to be preferred to the large number of special kinds that may be recommended. It is made like an ordinary flat shoe, but requires a longer piece of iron. The ends of the branches are bent inward over a dull corner of the anvil, are bevelled, laid one over the other, and welded to form the bar. The bar should be as wide and thick as the rest of the shoe, but slightly concaved on the side of the frog.

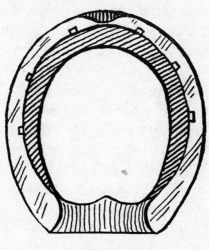

Fig. 35

This form of shoe is valuable for the reason that it protects certain sections of the wall from pressure, permits part of the body weight to be borne by the frog, and restores activity to disused parts of the foot. It may give a larger bearing surface for the hoof. By adding a leather sole to the bar shoe we may distribute the weight over the entire base of the foot, and this is desirable whenever the wall is not strong enough to bear the weight alone.

To make the leather sole and fasten it in place there must be holes in the ends of the branches, to which the leather is firmly riveted with small nails. The shoe should be wider than the hoof, and the clips higher than usual. The shoe is first fitted. Then the grooves for the clips are cut out of the leather, and the leather is riveted to the shoe, all projecting portions being cut away. The cleft of the frog and other cavities of the sole are then smeared thick with wood-tar and filled with oakum in such a way that the packing will bear part of the weight. The packing is of importance because it prevents slime and sand from filtering in, and preserves the horn, breaks the shock, and produces a gradual expansion of the back of the foot. Before the shoe is nailed on the leather sole should be soaked in water.

"Nailing." Wounds to the sensitive tissue caused by nails driven into the hoof for fastening shoes are usually spoken of under the general term "nailing." We distinguish direct and indirect nailing, according as the effects are felt at the time or later.

In direct nailing the nail penetrates the tender inner skin and always causes bleeding, even if blood is not observed. In extreme cases the coffin bone is chipped.

In the case of indirect nailing, the nail does not puncture the tender skin but passes very near to it and crowds the soft horn against the velvety tissue. This bulging presses on the pododerm and causes inflammation and lameness, which may not develop for several days.

Direct nailing causes instant pain, shown by jerking the limb, etc., and then more or less bleeding. Usually the blood flows from the nail-hole, or blood may be seen on the point of the nail; but internal bleeding may take place without any sign. In indirect nailing there is no immediate pain, often not for a day or two, but sometimes as soon as the horse bears his weight on the foot. In the latter case, when the other foot is raised the animal will throw his weight on the workman, or become restless. But usually pain does not develop for two or three days, and sometimes not for a week or two. In cases of that kind a careful examination will reveal internal inflammation of the hoof, increased warmth, some swelling of the hoof, and pain when the hoof is tapped or pressed with the pincers. Nailing may be suspected in all cases if the shoeing has been recent, if the hoof is small and narrow for the weight, if the walls have been thinned, or the nails driven very high or irregularly.

The most usual cause is an error in shoeing, chiefly a disregard of the *rule that nails should penetrate the white line.* Leading causes are: 1. Using badly punched shoes; 2. excessive paring and shortening of the hoof; 3. weakening the lower border too much by paring away on the outside; 4. mistakes in fitting the shoe, such as using shoes too narrow, letting the toe-clips penetrate the horn too far (by which the nailing around the toe, instead of penetrating the white line, is carried back to the sole), or using shoes in which the nailholes are improperly directed; 5. using nails that are split, or badly formed or bevelled, or that are too large; 6. starting nails with the bevel on the outside, or drawing them too tight. Sometimes the cause is old nail stubs in the horn, thin or broken walls, or a soft and crumbling wall which makes it difficult to know how the nail is being driven, or restlessness of the animal while being shod.

When nailing is suspected, tap the clinches, or press upon the sole and clinches with the hoof-testers, and if this causes pain there can be little doubt that "nailing" is the trouble.

Carefully draw each nail separately till the shoe can be removed, and examine each nail for blood stains or marks of pus, etc. Then look on the sole for the nailholes, and if one be found inside the white line, it is very probable that the nail driven there has caused the injury. Test every nailhole by passing a clean, new nail into it and pressing the point toward the soft tissues from time to time. Any sign of pain is a good indication of "nailing." Of course the nailholes in the shoe should be carefully examined.

Treatment for Nailing. In case of an ordinary prick with a nail, leave the nailhole empty and fill with wax. In most cases no serious trouble will follow. In case of serious direct nailing, a most careful examination of the entire shoeing should be made, especially noting if any nail passes inside the white line. More or less inflammation is to be expected, and this should be provided for by resting the animal and cooling the foot.

A clean recent wound can never be helped by enlarging the opening, or cutting or boring the horn. On the contrary, this will produce further injury.

In cases of indirect nailing, the results of which are not observed for some days, it will be observed when the injurious nail is withdrawn that it is covered with pus or a dark, thin, bad-smelling liquid. In all such cases the liquid must be allowed to escape freely. To do this it is usually sufficient to cut away a portion of the wall about the nailhole, not more than the thickness of the little finger, and then place the foot in a warm bath to assist in the discharge. It is a great mistake to remove all the loosened horn. After the liquids have passed away, the old horn will form the best dressing for the diseased region till new horn is formed.

If when the nail and pus have been removed, the pain does not cease, the foot should be placed in a bath about 90° in temperature, with an infusion of hayseed and a three to five per cent solution of carbolic acid in water. The bath must be kept really warm.

If the pain has been alleviated by two or three hot baths, a few drops of tincture of myrrh may be placed on the wound and the opening closed with carbolized oakum or cotton.

A horse that has been nailed will be ready for service again in a few days if he is provided with a shoe which does not press upon the inflamed region. *The shoe does not press when it rests only upon the bearing edge of the wall,* while the white line and sole are entirely free. Of course no nails can be driven near the inflammation.

Though usually not serious, nailing *may* produce lock-jaw which is nearly always fatal to a horse. It is always possible that nailing, however insignificant, may cause death.

Street Nail. When any sharp object in the street causes injury to the sole or frog, or lower bones or articulations, it is spoken of under the general name "street nail." Hind hoofs are most frequently affected. The chief point of entrance is the cleft of the frog, and is usually the result of thinning the sole or frog excessively.

The first symptom is usually sudden pain and lameness. If the cause proves to be a nail, piece of glass, or other object, it must be carefully drawn out, care being taken to leave no broken pieces in the foot. Always preserve the object drawn out, in case the doctor may wish to see it (if a doctor is called).

The sole may be thinned for an inch or so around the wound, but the opening would not be opened farther. Then cooling applications should be made. Deep, painful wounds require the attention of a doctor.

Usually a dressing of some kind is required, and this is to be held in place by a special shoe In most cases a simple splint dressing is sufficient The hoof side of an ordinary shoe is well concaved, and splints of tough wood firmly wedged between the hoof and the shoe. In special cases a covered shoe may be required. This has a sheet-iron cover, with a projection at the toe fitting into a corresponding indenture in the shoe, while at the heels it is fastened by screw heel calks.

Calking. This is the usual name for wounds to the coronet caused by the calks on the opposite foot, or by the shoes of other horses. A bruise on the coronet results in an interruption of the formation of horn at that point, making a cleft in the wall. The resulting lameness can be affected in shoeing only by shortening the wall under the affected part so that it will not press upon the shoe.

Corns. All bruises of the sole are usually spoken of as "corns," and appear as yellowish or reddish discolorations of the horn or white line. In most cases there is a rupture of the small blood vessels, causing a sort of blood blister under the horn. The staining of the horn is due to the blood penetrating the horn tubes. As the horn grows these patches are carried downward, and finally come to view on paring the hoof.

The usual place where corns appear is near the heels, often in the angles between the bars and the wall, or in the bars themselves. We distinguish corns of the sole, wall, and bars.

Corns chiefly affect the front hoofs, most often the inner half. Unshod feet are seldom affected. There are three kinds of corns: 1. Dry, in which the red-stained horn is dry, seldom accompanied by lameness; 2. Suppurating Corns, the result of a serious bruise followed by the formation of pus which is either thin and dark gray in color, indicating superficial inflammation of the pododerm, or thick and yellow indicating a deep inflammation causing lameness; 3. Chronic Corns, causing discoloration in all possible hues. The horn is soft and moist or crumbling and sometimes bloody. The inner surface of the horn is covered with horny swellings, and sometimes the coffin bone becomes enlarged and loosened. The gait is short and cautious; but when the shoe presses on the corn or the hoof gets dry, lameness follows.

The causes of corns are bad dressing of the hoof and faulty shoes. If wide, flat hoofs are too much trimmed, or the heels or bars or frog of other hoofs are weakened, the toe is usually left too long and corns follow. Shortening one heel more than the other, thus unbalancing the foot, is a frequent cause. Hollowing the sole excessively and thinning the heels are also often to blame. So, too, shoes not level on the hoof surface, shoes too short in the branches, or shoes which do not cover the bearing surface of the wall, result in corns in many cases. Another fault tending in the same direction is insufficient concaving; and shoes that become loose and get shifted produce similar injuries. In rare cases corns result from stones wedged between the frog and the branches of the shoe.

Dryness particularly favors the formation of corns and first shows itself by a short, cautious gait when the horse is put to work.

Treatment of Corns. First remove the cause. In an acute-angled hoof the toe is likely to be too long and should be shortened. If the quarters are too high they should be shortened, and care should be taken that the shoe that is fitted does not interfere with the elasticity of any part of the foot. Special care should be taken that the ends of the branches do not rise, and that in no case does the shoe press upon the sole.

In case of a suppurating corn, the shoe should be left off for a few days, and then a bar-shoe put on, as this best protects the bruised parts from being pinched.

Chronic corns should be permanently protected from any pressure from the shoe by using a leather sole on a bar-shoe. Blood-stained horn should not be dug out, but the whole region thinned, avoiding injuring the sensitive tissue or drawing blood. The hoof should be kept cool and moist.

Inflammation of the Bulbs of the Heels. This is due to external bruising, and may occur on shod or unshod feet. We will find swelling and increased warmth, sometimes signs of blood, and a short cautious gait or well marked lameness in case only one foot is affected.

Such inflammation is due to going barefoot on hard ground, shoeing feet with low heel bulbs with shoes that are too short, too much pressure on the frog by the bar of a bar-shoe, or forging and grabbing.

First, cool by applying an ice poultice or soak in cold water. Later drying applications will help, especially if the frog-band has been loosened from the bulbs of the heels, as for instance a weak solution of sulphate of copper (one part sulphate to twenty of water) and fitting shoes with heel calks and making them long in the branches and without pressure on the walls at the heels.

Founder. This is inflammation of the pododerm due to chilling as a direct result of excessive work or long standing in the stable. Often the entire shape of the hoof is changed, and

the disease is very painful.   In most cases both
fore feet are affected—very rarely only one foot
or all four feet.   When all the feet are affected,
traveling is nearly impossible, and there is a
high fever of the whole body.

The disease usually finds its seat in the fleshy
leaves of the toe, sometimes on the side walls
toward the heels.   As the inflammation pro-
ceeds the fleshy leaves are separated from the
horny leaves, the position of the coffin bone
changes, and the coronet of the toe sinks, and
the form of the hoof is changed.   It becomes
too high at the heels, rings form upon the walls,
and these rings show the course of the disease.
At the toe they are close together, gradually
separating toward the heels.   The wall of the
toe is sunken under the coronet, and the toe
itself is pushed forward.   In time the white
line is widened, and becomes dry and crumbling
so that a crack is liable to form between the
sole and the wall, leading to the formation of a
hollow wall.

If the inflammation does not occur too often
and disappears, no unnatural result follows
except that the horn remains rather brittle
afterward. If the inflammation is severe or
often repeated, the sole is flattened just in front
of the frog as a result of the sinking of the

coffin bone, and may even drop below the level
of the wall. In some cases the coffin bone will
even penetrate the sole in front of the point of
the frog, and the wall of the toe becomes permanently deformed. Skilful veterinary care
may remove the inflammation and prevent the
results described; but if this is not accomplished permanent deformity of the horny hoof
is inevitable.

A foundered horse can be used, but its gait
is extremely stiff and short, and the heels touch
the ground before the toe. This manner of
travelling wears off the branches of the shoe
with great rapidity.

In dressing such a foot, the thick projecting
wall at the toe may be removed without injuring the hoof; the sole may be pared, and the
whole hoof trimmed to give a correct bearing
on the ground.

If the sole is still concave, the regular shoe will
answer; but if it is flat or dropping, it should
be protected by a shoe with a broad web and a
bar, as shown in Fig. 36. This kind of shoe
is especially useful when the bearing surface of
the wall is broken or weak.

As long as the toe is affected, there should
be no toe clip, but two side clips, as shown in
Fig. 36. The wall between these clips should

be lower, not over an eighth of an inch, to prevent pressure on the sensitive parts. To prevent the shoe from working forward, as it often does in cases of this kind, clips should be raised at the ends of the branches or in the middle of the bar.

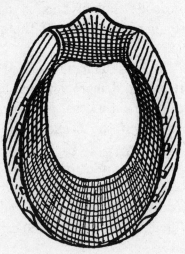

Fig. 36

Horn Tumor. This is of rare occurrence, and is not certainly indicated unless it extends down to the edge of the wall and causes a half moon-like bending inward of the white line that is waxen color, followed by crumbling of the wall. It may not cause lameness, and can be removed only by a veterinary doctor. In shoeing, carefully concave the shoe so as to remove all pressure from the inflamed region.

CHAPTER VII.

Flat Hoof and Dropping Sole. Horses bred on marshy ground are likely to have hoofs of which the side walls and toe are very oblique to the ground, while the sole is level with the bearing surface of the wall and the frog is highly developed. The branches of the sole sink even beyond the level of the wall.

In shoeing, remove the loose horn and level the deficient bearing surface of the wall, strongly rounding off the outer border, shortening the toe, and removing outward bendings of the lower border. The shoe should be of wide web and thick, with a bearing surface just corresponding to the edge of the wall, and sloping inward, while the shoe is well concaved, especially on the inner branch. The bearing surface of the branches must, however, be horizontal. If the hoof is otherwise defective, a bar-shoe will be required.

If the sole bulges beyond the edges of the wall, the only preparation needed for shoeing will be removal of loose horn. In some cases the bearing surface of the wall may be built up with hoof cement. The shoe should be light and broad in the web, with deep concaving (as circumstances require), extending from the inner edge of the web to the outer edge of the shoe and corresponding in shape to the bulge of the sole. A bar-shoe is to be preferred, and toe and heel calks are to be used to remove the sole sufficiently from the ground. The nails should be thin and long, and two side clips make the shoe more firm.

Flat and dropping soles cannot be cured, and shoeing can do nothing more than render such horses serviceable. Sensitive soles should be smeared with crude turpentine or pine tar. In cases of unusual sensitiveness, a leather sole should be fitted.

Never drive a horse with dropping soles faster than a walk over rough roads. During wet weather the soles should be smeared with hoof-ointment containing rosin to prevent softening.

Stumpy Hoof. In a hoof of this character the wall at the heels is too high for the toe, and the toe stands very steep. It arises from various affections (such as spavin) which tend to remove the heels from contact with the ground, or from neglect of horses running barefoot, or from shortening the toe too much.

If the position comes from the natural shape of the limbs, the hoofs should not be altered; but if from disease of the flexor tendons, etc., causing drawing up of the heels, the hoof should be properly treated until the heels are brought down. This may be done by sparing the wall at the heels, as by the use of thickened branches or calks. There is a tendency to wear off the toe, and if the work is hard on trying streets, a steel plate may be welded on the toe, especially of the hind hoofs. The shoe should also be bevelled outward a little making a wide base at the toe, have a strong toe clip, and be well concaved and rolled at the toe.

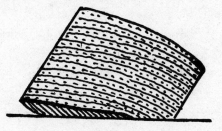

Fig. 37

In case the stumpiness is from neglect, the hoofs may be dressed in the ordinary way, and if the work is not heavy, the hoofs may be shod with tips as shown in Fig. 37, or with shoes of which the shanks have been thinned.

Contracted Hoof. The term contracted hoof

indicates a hoof which for any reason is too narrow toward the heels. The wall runs obliquely downward and inward. Sometimes only one side is contracted. Usually the angles are much prolonged and press on the frog, which shrinks, and the bars run in outward circles. Contraction is most often found on front feet, especially those with acute-angled toe. If the frog is found to be narrow and the fissures narrow and deep, there can be no doubt that the hoof is contracted.

The causes of contraction are lack of exercise, weakening the hoof toward the heels and leaving the toe too long, or neglecting to remove spurs of horn that press upon the frog. It is also caused by using shoes with branches wide apart, or inclined downward and inward so that the weight of the body squeezes the heels together.

Treatment. Remember that anything that exercises a moderate pressure on frog, sole, or bars tends to expand he hoof; hence frog and sole pads are to be recommended. Contracted hoofs cause nearly all the diseases of the foot, such as corns, thrush, bar-cracks, etc., and therefore every effort should be made to prevent them. Use flat shoes with a perfectly horizontal bearing surface in the branches,

and give abundant exercise, allowing the horse
to go barefoot as often as possible.

In very severe cases of contraction, if the
feet are not acute-angled, an expansive shoe,
with clips at the ends of the branches to press
upon the angles, is to be recommended. Under
no conditions use the expanding-screw except
under the advice of a doctor.

If the hoof is acute-angled, use the bar-shoe,
and if necessary even leather sole and foot-
packing. If the frog is foul it should be well
cleansed and disinfected with pine tar thinned
with alcohol or crude wood vinegar.

In addition we would recommend applying
tips, using shoes the bearing surface of whose
branches inclines downward and outward (or
if the contraction is on only one side, but a
single branch may be thus inclined); using
hoof-pads of rubber, straw, rope, cork, or hoof-
cement.

Sometimes wide hoofs are contracted, and
the contraction shows in a groove just under
the coronet, especially near the heels, but sometimes extending all around the hoof. Pain
is produced by tapping the contracted portion.s
Horses fresh from the pasture are very liable to
this form of contraction, and as a rule lameness
does not disappear entirely until the wall has re-

sumed its natural position once more. The wall
under the contracted portion should be lowered
so that it will not receive direct pressure, and
the bar-shoe should be used.

Sometimes the contraction is of the sole, and
the hoof curves from the coronet outward
and then inward, like a claw. The sole is ex-
ceedingly concave, and the bearing surface of
the wall is lessened from toe to heel. The cause
is usually dryness and lack of exercise, and
shoes whose bearing surface is not horizontal.
Flat shoes perfectly horizontal should be used,
with strong clips at the ends of the branches.

In all forms of contraction abundant exercise and daily washing are a necessary part of
the treatment.

Wry Hoofs. These are hoofs of which one
side is slanting and the other steep. We have
already considered those forms of wry hoofs
resulting from the position of the limbs as base-
wide or base-narrow, and contraction of one
side from disease. We will here consider wry
hoofs caused by shortening one wall too much
in shoeing.

The general rule is, cut down the oblique
wall and spare the steep wall. This is just the
reverse of the treatment of wry hoofs due to
misshapen limbs, for in this case the wryness of

the hoof does not correspond to the limb. To take the weight from the steep wall we may use a bar-shoe and concave the upper surface of the bar under the outer branch of the frog. The steep wall should not even rest upon the shoe, or in any way be attached to it. It should be left entirely free, either by cutting down the wall itself, or beating down the upper surface of the shoe.

Any sort of shoe may be used, though a flat shoe is best. If the foot has been improperly pared and we cannot rectify this at once, we may use a shoe with a thicker branch for the steep side. Colts with wry hoofs can often be cured by the simple process of correct shoeing. We use a shoe thick beneath the contracted wall, but gradually growing thinner around the toe to the end of the other branch. In some cases the branch may even end at the middle or the side wall. This shifts the weight of the body to the slanting wall and corrects the bad shape in three or four months.

Crooked Hoofs are such as are so bent that the bearing surface does not lie in proper relation to the coronet. They are caused by leaving one half of the wall too high, or by using normal shoes on hoofs of horses whose legs have the base-wide position.

The hoof should be so pared as to remedy this defect as much as possible, and then the shoe set out beyond the wall that is curved in so that a straight edge from the coronet will pass the curvature and touch the edge of the shoe. The opposite wall that is curved inward should be rasped down at the bearing edge until a straight line will touch all the way from the coronet to the shoe. Several shoeings will be required to rectify the shape of the hoof.

Side-bone (ossification of the lateral cartilage) is hardening of the cartilage under the bulbs of the heels into bone, and the disease is incurable. It is found most often in heavy horses, and causes lameness due to interference with the free movements of the foot. When advanced it causes a marked bulging of the coronet near the heels, and the protuberance is hard. The gait is short, and lameness follows hard work.

Special shoeing is helpful only when the outer cartilage is ossified and the hoof is contracted on that side. It will usually be found that the outer branch of the old shoe is more worn than the inner, and the outer wall will be found too high. This is due to the fact that the horn of the wall does not wear against the shoe, expansion and contraction having been interfered

with. A flat shoe is preferable, and the outer branch should be wider than the inner. The inner branch should follow the wall of the hoof closely, while the outer branch is full, toward the heels extending beyond the hoof. The shoe must of course be punched deep on the outer and fine on the inner branch, and a side clip should be placed on the outer branch. Bar-shoes are injurious in a case of this kind.

Cracks. We distinguish toe-cracks, side-cracks, bar-cracks, and heel-cracks. In the upper border of the hoof we find coronary cracks, while the cracks lower down are called low cracks; and the cracks may be deep, passing through the wall, or superficial.

Cracks are due largely to dryness and over-work on hard streets. Coronary cracks are the most serious and often cause lameness. The borders of the cracks *never* grow together, and are to be remedied only by healthy horn growing down from the coronary band.

Treatment of Cracks. In case of serious coronary cracks the horse should be allowed to go barefoot. The use of the bar-shoe (if shoes are necessary) is advised for all forms of crack, since it protects the diseased portion of the wall from pressure. If other diseases are present, the leather sole may be added. Coronary cracks should be fastened together by various means, such as, 1. Nails which rivet the crack together, the holes for the nails having been previously drilled; 2. Clamps forced into pockets burnt into the horn on opposite sides of the crack; 3. A thin plate of iron placed over the crack and secured by small wood screws; 4. wood screws screwed at right angles through the crack; 5. A strap buckled round the hoof.

In all cases care should be taken that the foot is so dressed that the shoe fits air-tight; but before the shoe is nailed on pressure on certain portions of the wall should be removed. In case of toe-cracks we may raise clips to press against the angles of the heels. Two side toe-clips may be drawn up, and the wall between them pared down.

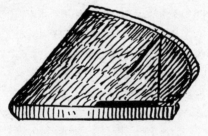

Fig. 38

In case of side-cracks, the portion of the wall between the extension of the horn tubes to the bearing surface and a perpendicular let down from the crack to the bearing surface should be lowered (Fig. 38).

In case of cracks toward the heels, use a bar-shoe and proceed as with side-cracks, even when the perpendicular line falls beyond the angles.

Hoof pads are of great value, since they distribute a part of the weight over the frog and sole.

When the crack is wide and the frog small, shoes with bar-clips may be used. If the edges of the crack are ragged and overlapping, the overlapping horn should be trimmed away. The horn over the coronary band on both sides of the crack should be thinned, and the coronet should frequently be moistened with laurel oil to guard against renewal of the crack.

In case of inflammation, poultices are recommended for several days. Fast trotting should be avoided till the sound horn has grown down at least two-fifths of an inch from the coronary band.

Bar-cracks occur only on the fore hoofs, and are due to contraction of the walls near the heels, or leaving the wall too high. They are usually accompanied by corns. If the crack extends to the pododerm, lameness will result and inflammation will set in which will extend to other parts of the foot unless promptly treated.

The portion of the hoof where the bars lie is so elastic that the cracks open and close with each step, and thus healing is made difficult.

Bar-cracks are usually not seen till the shoe is removed, and they then appear as dark streaks sometimes bloody or marked with hoof pus.

The horn in the vicinity of the crack should be pared very thin, and the edges of the crack cut away, and pressure on this part of the wall should be removed. The wall near the heel should be lowered and a bar-shoe used. When the crack has been pared down, a deep groove will appear, and if this is moist at the bottom the crack should be packed with oakum wet with myrrh or tincture of aloes, while the oakum should be sealed over with grafting wax.

Low cracks are usually caused by insufficient rounding of the bearing edge of the wall, in case of barefoot horses. They may also be caused by too large nails in shoes punched too near the edge. All that is necessary by way of treatment is proper shoeing. The bearing edge of the horn under the crack may be cut away in a half moon, and to prevent the crack from extending higher, the upper end of the fissure should be burnt out hollow or cut out with a hoof knife nearly to the inner leafy layer of horn.

Clefts are cracks at right angles to the horn

tubes, and are most frequent on the inner toe and side as a result of injury from sharp heel calks improperly placed, though they may come from suppuration. The shoer can do nothing in cases of this kind, except to drive no nails in the horn below the cleft (to avoid breaking it off), and by shortening the wall below. If, however, the horn is loose, it should be removed and the fissure filled with grafting wax or horn cement.

Loose Wall is separation of the wall from the sole along the white line. It is most frequent on fore hoofs and on the inner side, especially when the foot is wide and flat.

Loose wall is caused by very slanting walls, outward bending of the bearing edge of the wall, burning the horn wih hot shoes, dryness, neglect of shoeing, excessive poulticing with cow dung, carelessness in preparing the bearing surfaces of the shoe, and uneven fitting of the shoe.

The causes of the looseness should of course be entirely removed and the wall properly shortened. Then we may use a shoe with the bearing surface inclined downward and inward. It should be smooth and wide enough to cover the bearing surface of the hoof as far in as the border of the sole. In case of lameness, we should use a bar-shoe or a leather sole. If the separation of the wall extends far, the wall should not be lowered, but the crack should be filled with wood tar, crude turpentine, or soft grafting wax. In case loose wall occurs on an unshod hoof, the loose portion should be entirely removed if possible; else the hoof should be shod. The hoof should be cared for by shoeing at least once a month and judicious moistening.

Hollow Wall may be suspected when a bulging outward of the wall is observed, which sounds hollow when tapped. It consists in separation of the wall from the sensitive tissues, and is quite rare. A crack will be seen in the white line, though the separation of the wall may be less in extent than the length of the crack. The cavity frequently extends to the coronet, and is filled with crumbling horn. Pain is not usual, but lameness may in some cases result. It is caused by chronic inflammation of the fleshy leaves. A cure is possible, but requires time. In shoeing, pressure should be removed from the hollow section of wall, the cavity cleansed and filled with tar, crude turpentine, or wax. If the cavity is extensive, a bar-shoe should be used.

Thrush of the Frog makes the horn of the frog ragged, and a bad-smelling, dark liquid collects in the cleft. In the course of several months the frog-band will be affected and irregular rings and cross rings will be formed on the wall. The cause is lack of exercise in the fresh air, or too great paring of the frog, removing the frog from the ground by heel calks, or the use of frog pads for several months in succession.

All the greasy horn of the frog should be removed, as well as the overgrown angles. The frog should be washed once or twice a day, exercise should be abundant, and shoes without aclks.

CHAPTER VIII.

SHOEING MULES AND OXEN.

The hoofs of mules and asses are similar to those of horses, but the hoof of a mule is longer, narrower, and round at the toe, the sole is well arched, and the side walls steep. The hoofs of asses are narrower and the wall relatively thicker, while the frog is well developed, making the hoof wide toward the heels. The horn of the hoofs of mules and ass is tough.

Shoes should be light and narrow. Four nails will hold on an ass's shos, five or six, a mule's. The nails should be short, but strong in the shank to prevent their bending.

Oxen require very different shoes from horses on account of the cloven hoof. The two pasterns and the hoof bone are double, one bone for each claw; and there is no frog. The wall and sole are thin, the bulbs of the heels low. A thin, wide shoe is therefore required, and there must be a separate shoe for each claw.

The holes must be punched near the edge and the nails should be short and strong. The shoe for each claw has a long tongue on the inner side that is turned upward and around the toe, and a small clip should be raised on the outer edge for further stability(Fig. 39).

An undivided or "close-claw" shoe is useful only for heavy work over rough roads where there is danger of straining the fetlock and coronary joints.

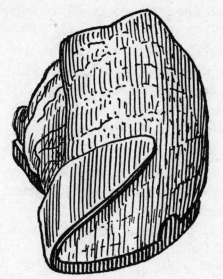

Fig. 39

There is always great difficulty in holding the feet of oxen while they are being shod. The head should be fastened to a tree, post, or wall, and a front foot may be held up by a slip-noose passed over the back at the withers and held by an assistant on the opposite side. In case of a hind limb, a pole may be placed in front of the hock and a man at each end of the pole may carry the leg back and up, where it should be held in place. Obstinate oxen may sometimes be controlled by giving a light blow with a stick at the base of the horns. If many oxen are to be shod, stocks will be found necessary. When no stocks are available we may use an ordinary farm wagon. Tie the ox with head between front and hind wheels. Fasten the large end of a binding pole to the spokes of the front wheel, letting it rest on the hub. Swing the pole to the side of the ox and under one hind leg, bringing it around to the side of the wagon and drawing it up till the leg swings nearly free. The pole may be fastened to the rack or other support. The most refractory oxen may be controlled in this way by two persons.

PART III.

CARRIAGE BUILDING

CHAPTER I.

CARRIAGE IRONING.

Carriage building is divided into three branches, to each of which one man usually devotes his attention. These are carriage-ironing, spring-making, and tire-welding; but a good smith should be master of all three or, in other words, he should be able to iron a carriage complete. (See Fig. 40).

Edge Plates. The first pieces of iron-work that are made for a carriage are edge plates. These consist of two flat iron plates from two to four inches in width, and from three-eighths to five-eighths of an inch thick, according to the size and description of the carriage, and they extend from the front to the back of the body. It is always the best plan to have the sides of the body in the shop to fit the plates

Fig. 40

to. Some of the corners may be turned, but
where extra strength is required, they should
be welded. The plates should be well fitted
down to the wood without burning. They are
best fitted in two or three pieces, and then
welded together, the length being taken with
a pair of compasses. If the plate is straight
edgewise over the weld, one mark on each piece
will be sufficient to take the length with; but
if the plate is convex or concave edgewise, then
two marks are necessary, one on either side of
the plate. Before the last weld is made—that
is, when the plate is in two pieces—the plate

should be perfectly fitted to within four inches of the place where it is to be welded, and should never be altered again after it is welded, except the few inches left unfitted over the shut. The holes which of necessity must be drilled should not be too far apart, but close enough to hold the plate firmly to the wood; yet they should not be so close as to weaken the plate.

The Wheel Plate. The edge plates disposed of, the next piece of iron-work that will be wanted is the wheel plate; and if the carriage is to be of modern design, the iron futchel and cap, or middle of front bar, and the perch-bolt. The dimensions of these must correspond to the carriage. The wheel plate is made in two pieces, and unless the bearings come very close together, it should be made of half-round iron, with a small flat edge, and upset to form the bearings; but if the bearings come close together then flat iron should be used, the space between the bearings being made half-round with a top tool. The bearings should be left one inch longer than they are required to be when finished, and one-sixteenth inch thicker on the intended outside than on the inside when the iron is in the straight, as in compassing they always draw on the outside edge and contract on the inside. A circle should be drawn in chalk on the fitting-plate, the diameter of the intended wheel plate, so as not to burn the pattern when compassing the half-round iron. Do not bruise the edges of the half-round iron any more than you can possibly help, or you will soon get into trouble with the viceman. The wheel plate when made should be a perfect circle, and perfectly flat on the flat side. If there is a sway-bar, it is usually made with the wheel plate of the same iron, and is about one-third of a circle of a much larger diameter than the wheel plate, behind which it is fixed, to give a larger bearing surface.

The futchel may be made in various forms and shapes, and nearly every firm of coach-builders has a different style, hence it would be impossible to lay down any definite rule for making this piece of iron-work.

The perch-bolt is so simple that it needs no description.

Bed Plates. While the carriage-maker is making the carriage, the springs should be made, a description of which will be given later on, and we will proceed with our ironing. The bed plates are next on the list. These consist of five plates, mostly half-round, and fitted to three peculiarly-shaped pieces of timber, the horn-bar, top bed, and bottom bed. The horn-bar plate is sometimes made flat and sometimes

half-round. If of the former style, it is of the
same width as the wood, and from a quarter
to three-eighths of an inch thick, drawn off to
one-eighth of an inch at the ends and fitted to
the back side of the horn-bar. If of the latter
style, it is usually one inch or one and one-eighth
wide, with a feather edge drawn off a little at
the end.

Top Plate. The top plate fits on the top
side of the top bed. It is half round with a
feather edge when finished, with flat bearings
on each end which support the body, and
a flat boss in the centre, with a square hole to
take the head of the perch-bolt. This plate
is best made of flat iron from an inch and a
half to two inches in width, and from one-half
to five-eighths of an inch thick, according to
the size of the carriage, upset in the middle to
form the boss, which should be one-eighth of an
inch thicker than the half-round when finished.
When the iron is upset, punch the square hole
and cut a little with a fuller to form the boss.
Next proceed to make the flat iron half round
with top tools, between the boss and the bearings, compassing edgewise as you proceed if
necessary. This, like all other plates, should
be well fitted down to the wood without burning. When finished the plate should be a little

under the width of the wood, except at the bearings, which should be the exact width of the wood.

The Transom Plate. The socket transom, or transom plate, is fitted on the top side of the bottom bed. It is somewhat shorter than the top plate, having bearings on each end on which the wheel-plate works. There is a socket welded in the centre in which works the perch-bolt. The socket is first made of a piece of flat iron $2\frac{1}{4}$ inches by $\frac{1}{4}$ inch, the ends are scarfed, bent round, and welded on a small beak-iron, or mandrel. When both ends of the socket are welded, form a scarf like the brim of a hat-box by hammering one end on the beak-iron, or on the back edge of the anvil, with a bob punch from the inside. Put a mandrel in the hole and round up in the tools and the socket is finished. Get a piece of flat iron a little heavier than that used for the top plate, upset in the middle where the socket is to be welded, punch a hole large enough to admit the socket, which must drive in tight, and it is then ready for welding. Have a bolster in which the socket fits nicely greased, and a mandrel that fits into the socket also greased. Get the heat well, but without burning the top of the socket. This heat must be worked very quickly, as there is a lot to do.

First, upset the end lightly; next, narrow in on the edge and compass if necessary; put the socket in the bolster and have a light, quick blow on the scarf, and, while it is still welding hot, insert the mandrel, knock off the bolster, and narrow in on theedge; knock out the mandrel, and form a boss around the socket with a fuller, like the top plate; then put the socket into the bolster again, and clean up with the flatter and set the mandrel square in the socket. This can all be done in one heat if worked quickly, and it is ready to be tooled like the top plate.

The boss plate is fitted on the bottom side of the top bed. It has no bearings except the boss in the centre, which works on the boss of the transom plate, the hole being left a little smaller than the diameter of the socket, to allow for fitting up by the viceman. This plate is also made of flat iron, the ends being drawn off thin and made half round with top tools.

The Bottom Plate. This plate is fitted on the bottom side of the bottom bed. It is generally made of very stiff half-round iron, ordered expressly for the purpose, and left much stronger than the other plates, this being the main support of the front part of the body, commonly called the "boot." It has a boss in the centre

like the other plates, to receive the nut of the
perch-bolt, and bearings at the ends to take the
springs. Sometimes there is a T-flap welded
on each end, that fits between the spring-block
and the wheel-iron head. At other times there
are butterfly flaps with holes to receive the spring
clips. The iron used for these flaps should be
twice the thickness the flaps are required to be
when finished. The beds and bed-plates are
concentric to each other, the perch-bolt passing
through the whole.

Wheel Irons and Front Bars. When the carriage-maker has got the carriage ready, the
wheel irons and front bar (if there be one)
may be made. These are the irons with a bolt
through the ends, which connect the shafts to
the carriage, and are made in a variety of different styles to suit the taste of the coach-
builder. The part which lips the bottom bed
on the spring bearing is termed the "head."
Some of these are made of flat iron, and the
round or oval iron welded on with a mitre, the
corners being turned. Others are made of
half-round iron, the round or oval iron being
drawn out of the half-round, and the corners
turned. Others, commonly called the "sugar-
loaf head," are made out of the solid of square
iron, in which cases the corners are not turned,

but the head is formed first by being cut in with a fuller and then worked up square with a top and bottom set. The back end of a wheel iron is termed the "tail" or "stag," and is made either round or oval, and is connected to the hind end of the futchel with a small boss or L-flap. If it is an iron futchel, the wheel irons are connected to the front bar, either with a splice or wood block, the splices being made separate and fitted up by the viceman before they are welded to the wheel-irons and front bar or cap, In the case of wooden futchels, the front bar is dispensed with, the futchel plates taking its place, and the front ends of the futchel connect it to the wheel-iron in the place of a block or splice. The wheels are shod next, a description of which is given farther on.

Thus far the carriage may be ironed while the body is being made. If the carriage is a landau, victoria, or phaeton, a set of head props will be required, and they are made after patterns furnished by the body-maker.

Head Irons. The head joints that lift the head up and down are usually patented and self-acting, and are made and fitted by workmen employed by the patentee.

Hind Irons. In the first place the carriage-maker, when the body is finished, makes the patterns of the pump-handles or hind irons which connect the hind springs and wheels to the body. These, like the wheel irons, are made in a variety of shapes. They are mostly made of square iron, from $1\frac{1}{4}$ inch to $1\frac{1}{2}$ inch; sometimes they are made of Bessemer steel, to admit of their being made very light. They take a bearing on the top of the spring about six inches long; this bearing is mostly half-round at the top, whilst the bearing that takes the body is half-round at the bottom; the space in between and the ends are oval. Sometimes, to prevent the pump-handles being cranked edgewise, a flap is welded on the inside to take the spring bearing. The flap is welded on while the iron is square, and should be five-eighths of an inch thick before being welded; this should clean up nicely to seven-sixteenths of an inch thick when finished. Weld this flap on soundly, and while still welding hot, apply the half-round or oval tools, as the case may be. Both flaps on, proceed to draw the ends off, and finish. Sometimes this style of pump-handle has a wooden casing on the top, which is artistically carved, in which case the top of the pump-handle is left flat and the bottom half-round.

Cross Spring. If the hind part of the car-

riage is to be hung on the side springs and top
halves, a cross spring and span-iron will be required. The latter spans the hind part of the
body above the cross spring. There is a T or
L-flap on each end, which fits on the front ends
of the pump-handles, for which purpose the ends
of the span iron often have to be cranked. The
iron between the centre bearing—which is about
six inches long and takes the cross spring—
and the flaps are mostly oval, and is made out
of one inch square iron, tooled on the angle.
The bearing is made separate, off a piece of flat
iron the width of the spring and about three
quarters of an inch thick, about three inches at
each end being made oval and welded on to
the other pieces when the ends are finished.
When the crank is very short (say one to two
inches deep) it is best turned before the flaps
are welded on; but when the cranks are deep
they may be turned afterwards. Although
the oval part of the span-iron is often very
much compassed and twisted, it will seldom
want any fitting in the wood-shop if it is set
true to the pattern when in the smith's shop,
provided, of course, the pattern is true to the
body.

Sometimes the span-iron is dispensed with,
and a small stay or bracket substituted, which

consists of a short piece of oval iron with a T-flap at each end, one to take the top of the cross-spring, while the other is bolted on the bottom of the body.

The axle-trees arrived from the makers, the springs made and fixed to the axle-trees, the carriage put together, and the wheels ready, the body may be now what is technically termed "hung" or mounted. The body steps may now be made. These also may be made in a number of different styles. They may be either branch tops or T-flaps, with plain treads or gridirons for the steps, or they may be self-acting, that is, opening and shutting with the door. This class of step has the advantage of being always clean for the person to tread on, and being self-acting, requires no folding up when the door is closed. But they are seldom used for any carriages except landaus, as they are expensive to make and finish.

Branch Steps. The branch steps are made of flat iron one inch by one-half or five-eighths, each step being made in one piece. The iron is cut off the required length and ovaled. The ends of both pieces are then put into the fire, and drawn off to form the flaps, which are half-round, about one and three-eighths inches wide, one foot, more or less, being left flat between the

ovals. One piece may now be dropped, as one
heat will require all the attention. The one
piece is heated in the middle between the ovals;
it is then bent double, the flat sides of both flaps
coming together. The joint here—the flat iron
—is made perfectly close, so as to be proof against
the admission of dirt. Some smiths put a small
piece of hoop iron in the joint at the crotch to
strengthen it, but this is to be avoided, as it is
very apt to fall out in the fire and give place to
dirt. But a shoulder may be formed on the inside when tooling in the first place, which is always preferable. A good welding heat is now
taken on the flat iron at the crotch, care be¹ng
taken not to burn the oval. When on the anvil
it is first welded up square, then the corners are
worked in, and then it is ovaled. The flap to
hold the tread is now made, or the gridiron welded on, as the case may be. This step is now
laid aside, and the other treated in the same
manner. When the latter is made like the former, it is bent out at the bottom, and then the
branch opened out as near as possible to the pattern while the iron is hot. This is then laid aside
while the other is bent and opened out in the
same manner. This one, in its turn, is laid aside
to cool, while the other,—which by this time is
cold enough to handle—is set true to the pattern.

This done, the other is also set true. They are
then ready to be fitted to the body.

Steps with T-Flaps. Steps with T-flaps are
somewhat plainer. A stump of inch or inch and a
quarter round iron is jumped onto a piece of flat
or half-round iron about an inch and a half wide
by five-eighths of an inch thick, about five inches
from the end, and welded in a bolster. It is cut
off five inches the other side of the stump and
another made in the same manner. The ends
are then drawn off half-round. These form the
flaps or top of steps. If the steps are to have
plain treads, the stump may be left long enough
to form the spade or flap to hold the tread;
but if the steps are to be very deep, and require
a long stem, it is advisable to weld on only a short
stump, and have a shut in the middle of the
stem, which may be either round or oval to order.
If the steps are to have gridiron treads, the frame
of the gridiron is, of course, made separate, the
bars being riveted in afterwards by the viceman.
A smaller stump is welded on a smaller piece of
iron than that used for the flaps, but in the same
manner. The iron intended for the frame is
drawn out half-round, one inch wide, and long
enough to make the whole frame. The corners
are then turned and the frame welded up, the
sides where the bars are to be riveted in being

left one inch wide, while the front and back are narrowed in to seven-eighths of an inch wide. When the frame is set square it is ready to be welded on the top part. These, like all other body steps, should be set true to the pattern, but they will always require a little fitting to the body afterwards.

The *Wings* are fitted over the wheels and covered with leather to catch the mud splashes. A hint or two on the forging will be sufficient. Have as few shuts as possible, upset the iron as little as possible, and never get into the habit of taking two welding heats to one shut. To this end the scarfs should be small and narrow.

The *Seat Rails* are made of round iron about one-half inch, and shaped to a pattern. Great care should be taken to get both sides the same height, and the back perfectly true with the seat board, so when it is fixed it is just a convenient height to catch the eye, and any little deviation from the square would be immediately detected, and if not altered would be a black mark against the smith who made it.

The *Dash Iron* is made of the same sort of oval iron as the wings, and is comparatively simple, the most difficult part being the flaps. A piece of flat iron about an inch and a quarter by half an inch is upset at one end, and split up edgewise and scarfed. It is then jumped on a piece of five-eighths or three-quarters inch round, about two inches from the end. This should be welded in one heat, and squared up with the set hammer and scarfed in the place where the upright over is wanted, then cut off about three inches the other side of the flap, and hold in a pair of tongs. The oval iron, having been cut off and upset, is welded on in one heat, and cleaned up in the oval tools. The three inches of round iron in the tongs is now made oval, and the two inches of the other side of the flap is drawn down to one half inch round, and a corner turned to form the bottom part of the handle. It is then laid aside, and the other made in the same manner. The middle is best made separate and welded to the sides after. The top piece of oval is next welded about two inches from the end onto the upright oval of one of the sides. A piece of seven-sixteenths inch round is now welded to the end of the top piece of oval, and the corner turned to form the handle. The top is now held in a pair of tongs, while the handle is welded at the bottom, the flap drawn off half round, and turned to the required angle. The other side is treated in the same manner, the middle is made and welded to the sides, and set true. A dash iron should not require any fitting, but when fixed it should be perfectly square with the seat rail. The boot-steps, bracket plates, front stays, hind pole socket, and lamp irons all follow in their turn, and are, of course, made to pattern.

The *Boot Steps* are somewhat smaller than the body steps, and are fixed on the side of the body just above the front wheels, and should always match the body steps.

The hind *Pole Socket* is merely a socket with two small stays to connect it to the carriage, to support the hind end of the pole when the carriage is drawn by a pair of horses. The lamp irons are two T-flaps welded to the sockets supplied with the lamps. The splint-bar and shaft plates are the only pieces of importance that remain to be made. The splint-bar plate is fitted on the bottom side of the bar. It is sometimes flat and sometimes half round. A front pole socket is fitted in the centre, and takes the two middle roller bolts. Sometimes the socket is made in the solid with the plate. In that case it is made separate and welded in. The two shaft plates are fitted on the bottom side of the shafts, and are made of half-round iron, flattened out and bent round the hind end that works in the futchel ends. They are drawn off thin at the front ends, and all the holes punched.

Springs. Carriage springs are usually made

in pairs, the front pair being made first. The smith must know: 1. The description of the spring; 2. the length of the spring and the compass: 3. the number of plates and the gauge number of steel to be used, the number of holes, and if more than one, the size and centres. The dimensions obtained, proceed to make out the measures in chalk on a piece of flat iron. Carriage springs are mostly elliptical, and when otherwise are made by the same rule, except the old-fashioned C springs, which are made to a pattern.

Suppose the order is for a pair of elliptical springs with cup heads, three feet three inches long, nine inches span, six plates, Nos. 2, 3, and 4 steel. These springs are suitable for the fronts of broughams, landaus, etc. It must be borne in mind that three feet three inches is to be the length of the springs when finished, so we must allow an inch and a quarter in our measure for what the steel will contract in compassing. Thus our measure must be three feet and four and a quarter inches. This is to be the length of the backs in the straight, to and from the centre of the holes in the eye or head. The next thing is to arrange the lengths of the various plates. The ends of the long plates should reach to the centres of the holes in the head, the next plate two and a half inches above that, the next plate two and seven-eighths inches above that, the next plate three and three-eighths inches higher, and the short plate four inches higher still. This will give you a short plate about 15¼ inches long.

Next cut down the steel No. 2 for the backs and short plates. No. 3 for the long plates, and No. 4 for all the other plates. The plates should draw about two and a half inches each end, therefore cut them down that much shorter. Allow two and a half inches for each eye and an inch and a half for each head.

Now that all is ready, proceed to roll the eyes. These may be made in one heat if worked quickly. Thin out the end of the steel on the front edge of the anvil, and roll a small, close eye. Insert a mandrel slightly tapered, and insert another the required size and quite parallel. Then with a punch that fits the eye, make the hole perfectly round by a light blow with the hand hammer. While these ends are cooling, make two of the heads.

The heads may be made in a number of different ways, the simplest and quickest being the best. This is as follows: Make a double clip off a piece of inch and an eighth or inch and a quarter half-round iron feather edge. Upset the steel well, not too close to the end, the clip being cold and the steel hot.   Thin the end of the steel a little, put on the clip, and drive the fangs well into the hot steel.   Then, with a nice clean, clear fire, take a good welding heat, without burning the steel.   The feather edge of the half-round iron will form a good scarf, and should weld up quite sound and clean the first heat.   Square it up with the set hammer, round the ends of the iron, and punch the holes, one square and the other round, little more than half way through from the inside.   Now take another welding heat, and work quickly with the hand hammer on the anvil, and while it is still welding hot, turn the lugs in the vice with a light, quick blow. The corners turned, pinch one of the lugs in the vice and draw the front of the head over the end of the vice with the hand hammer.   Serve the other lug the same.   Now take another welding heat, and put a fuller, the width of the steel and about half an inch thick, in the head, and with a light, quick blow, form the cup in which the eye is to fit.   The holes are now punched through from the outside.   A temporary eye, the width of the spring, is put into the head, and the lugs closed.   A mandrel, square at the top and round at the bottom, is driven through the hole.   It is then put in the vice, and the top of the head worked up square with the hand hammer. The steel behind the head is cleaned up with a flatter. It may now be got hot and filed on the top with a rasp or coarse-cut file, and the head is finished. The other is made in the same manner.

While these two heads are cooling, roll the other two eyes. Apply the measure first to see how much steel the first two eyes have taken up; then allow the same amount for the other two.

Open heads are made in a somewhat different style. A piece of flat iron an inch by three-quarters or seven-eighths square, is bent round about three inches from the end in the shape of a hook. The end at the bend is then scarfed with a fuller and welded onto the steel, which has previously been upset and scarfed. The iron is then cut off the length of the end that has been turned, and the corners and inside of the head worked up square with a small set. Another welding heat is taken to secure any little scarf that may have been opened in the working up, and the lugs are finished to the shape required. The holes in these heads are best drilled, as they may then be placed to a nicety.

The heads and eyes finished, proceed to build

a hollow fire with wet small coal, and when ready, commence to draw the plates.

The points of the plates should not be welding hot when taken out of the fire, but a nice white heat. A plate should be drawn from just above where the point of the next plate will come, and drawn out very thin at the points. The slits for the studs to work in should be punched in such a position that the points of the next plate come one inch past it. Each point should be drawn and finished in one heat. Draw one end of all the plates first; then apply the measure, cut off any superfluous steel, and mark the plates Nos. 1, 2, 3, and 4 with a centre punch or the corner of the cold chisel. Then draw the other ends.

When all the backs and plates are studded, the backs are hardened and tempered in the following manner: Heat No. 1 bottom back from end to end to a light red heat. Compass on the anvil a little more than is actually needed, so that, in setting, as few blows as possible may be struck on the face side, which has to be filed bright. Then plunge it in clean water. Now proceed to temper for let down the hardened back by drawing it slowly through the fire till a piece of dry stick will blaze freely when rubbed on the hot part. An old hammer shaft answers very well for this purpose. The other backs are tempered and hardened in the same manner when required. The heads and eyes need not be hardened at all, or if hardened, should be annealed after. Next set the back straight edgewise, if necessary, by holding it flat on the anvil and drawing with the hand hammer on the contracted edge. The blows must not be struck too near the edge to damage it, but close enough to have the desired effect. Now set the back to the proper compass over the vice, and take out the flat places in the sweep. The compass of the back when finished should be about two and a half inches, and the plates should spring enough when finished to bring it up to four and a half inches, the required compass.

The backs must be set square with a pair of steel squares or winding sticks. Great care should be taken in this operation.

The viceman should file out the slits to fit the studs so that the plates will lay true on each other. We next proceed to harden and fit the plates. Three pairs of spring pliers will now be required for the purpose of pinching in, as it is technically termed. Heat the long plate marked No. 1 to a red heat—a little hotter than the backs—the back also marked No. 1 being ready on the fitting plate. Place the hot plate in position, and pinch it in close to the back, as quickly as possible. With one pair of pliers in each hand, lift the back with the plate upon end, and pinch the lower end in the vice. The blow-boy holds the two together at the top with one pair of pliers, while the smith and viceman, each with a pair of pliers, pinch the hot plate well into the back, beginning at the top and working downward. This should be repeated twice, and the plate immediately released and cooled quickly. In short, the whole must be done very rapidly, or the plate will be too cold when dipped to harden. Temper the plate in the same manner as the back, and fit it to the back both flat and edgewise.

It is advisable to finish one half of one spring first, and put it together and try the compass. If it is right, the spring may be taken apart to make the others by. The long plate should have more spring than any of the others, the spring getting less and less as the plates get shorter. The last should not have more than a quarter of an inch. When finished, the spring should be a perfect sweep on top, without a break.

Tires. The only information needed by a smith about to shoe a set of wheels is the size of the iron for the tires and the stock-hoops.

The wheels are marked No. 1 and No. 2, the iron for the tires laid flat on the ground, one wheel placed on one end of the iron, and a chalk mark put on the wheel where the end of the iron comes. The wheel is then rolled along the iron and the holes marked, one on each side of the felloe joints, till the chalk mark on the wheel comes round to the bar again. A mark is made at this point. This is the dead length, so three-quarters of an inch to an inch, according to the size of the tire, must be allowed beyond this for what the iron will contract in bending. The tire is marked the same number as the wheel, and the others treated in the same manner. The ends of the bars are cut off, the holes centre punched, and the ends bent a little about one foot over the beak iron. They are then taken to the bending machine. This, in most shops, is merely a piece of stiff, flat iron bent convex, with a piece of small flat iron about one inch by half an inch welded over the end in the form of a bridge about one inch high. This is fixed by two or three suitable stays to a wall or pillar, about five or six feet from the ground.

The end of one of the bars is put on the compassed iron, the end catching under the bridge. The other end is pulled down, lifted again, and pushed farther through the bridge, and pulled

down again; and so on to the end. When the
end gets too short to be pulled down by the
hand, a wrench or lever is applied. The front
tires being smaller than the hind, a wedge piece
is put on the top of the convex iron and the tire
bent over that, thus making a smaller circle.

This done, one of the tires is laid flat on the
wheel plate, which should always be perfectly
level. The flat or quick places are taken out of
the circle with a quarter hammer and dolly,
and the tire is set flat or edgewise to the wheel
plate.

When the wheels have all been treated in this
manner, the two front wheels are run with a
traveler. This is a circle cut out of a piece of
flat sheet iron about six inches in diameter with
a hole in the centre for a rivet to hold the handle,
which should clip the traveler on each side like
a fork, as closely as possible, to admit of the
traveler working freely and true.

The wheel marked No. 1 is laid on the anvil
and a large bolt or mandrel put through the hole
in the wheel and the hole in the anvil. A chalk
mark is put on the edge of the wheel, and a notch
for a starting point cut in the traveler with a
file. The traveler is then applied to the wheel,
the marks being opposite each other, and the
wheel turned round with the left hand, while

the traveler is held to the wheel with the right. When the wheel is turned round once, a chalk mark is put on the traveler corresponding with the mark on the wheel. This side of the traveler is marked No. 1. The other front wheel is run in the same manner, the mark being put on the other side of the traveler. The front tire marked No. 1 is now lodged on the anvil and forge. The smith gets inside, and having set the notch to the right end, runs the traveler round the tire. The chalk mark on the traveler should come to the other end of the tire. This will admit of one-half inch being cut off each of the four corners before scarfing. If the chalk mark on the traveler runs short of the end, the tire is too long, so must have a piece cut off. If, on the other hand, the chalk mark runs beyond the end, the tire is too short, so must not be further shortened.

Now put the ends of the tire into a clean fire, and when hot cut what may be necessary off the corners. Scarf the ends with a fuller, and close them. Bend the tire to give a little spring to hold the scarf together. Now take a good welding heat and finish the shut. This done, put a chalk mark on the tire and run round with the traveler.

If the tire is, say, an inch and a half by half

an inch, and the joints in the felloes are closed up, the tire should be left half an inch smaller than the wheel; but if the joints are left open at all, the tire should be left from five-eighths to seven-eighths of an inch smaller than the wheel. The hind tires are left five-eighths to an inch smaller than the wheel.

The holes are now drilled not quite through with a taper drill, just so that the drill pricks through. The hole is then punched through with a small hand punch. Sometimes the holes are not drilled till the tires are on the wheels.

The tires are now ready for the furnace, where they are heated all over to a blood heat. While the tires are heating, one of the wheels is screwed down to the wheel plate, the back side uppermost, and some thin wedges are put under the felloes on the outside to keep the tire from dropping too far on the wheel.

Two dogs or wrenches are required to pull the tire on with, and a quarter hammer to give a blow if necessary, and two water buckets filled with water to cool the tire as quickly as possible. A sinking platform permitting the whole wheel to be lowered into a tank of water is better.

The tire should be blood hot all over, not black in places. When taken out of the furnace it is picked up by the smith and hammerman with two pairs of tongs.   One side is put on the wheel, while the hammerman pulls the other over with the dogs, and the smith taps it on with the hammer.   It is then cooled, and when nearly cold is taken up off the wheel plate and set to the wheel or rather the wheel is set to the tire with a wooden mallet.

When putting the tire on, be sure the holes are in their right position.   The tire should not require much hammering on, as it is very apt to split the felloes.   If it will not go on and it is the right size, it must be because it is not hot enough, so it should be made hotter.

If there is no furnace in the shop, the tires have to be blown hot on the forge, which is very inconvenient and takes much more time.   In that case the tire is laid on the forge so that one part is in the fire.   The fire is then covered up with coal, and the tire is covered up with bricks, wood, and shavings.   The tire is blown hot, and continually turned round with a wrench till it is hot all over.

If there is more than one set of tires to be put on, they should all be welded up first, so that once heating the furnace will do for the lot.

The stock hoops are next made.   The length of iron required may be got by multiplying the diameter of the stock by three and adding one-seventh. Thus if the diameter of the stock was seven inches, 7x3=21x1=22 inches. Again, if the diameter of the stock is six inches, 6x3=18x$\frac{7}{8}$inch=18$\frac{7}{8}$, which is near enough for all practical purposes. Greater accuracy may be obtained by multiplying the diameter by 3.1416, the relation between the diameter and circumference of all circles.

A smith accustomed to the work will not need to upset the ends; but one not accustomed to the work will require a half inch beyond the dead length to upset. The back hoops are easy enough, but the front hoops require a little skill and attention when in the fire or a piece will be burnt out of one edge before the middle is red hot. They must be worked very quickly when hot, as the heat is soon lost. They always have a tendency to turn up on the edges and leave a hollow place in the middle. This should be carefully avoided, as it is almost impossible to get rid of this hollow place once it appears, and to this end draw it more in the middle than on the edges. When they are welded sound, round them up on a mandrel or beak-iron. Put the back hoops on warm and file them. File the front hoops before putting them on, and drive them on cold, as they have two nails to hold them.

CHAPTER II.

As this is primarily a book on blacksmithing, we will not go into elementary carpentry, and it is assumed that any one who attempts to build the woodwork of a carriage will be to some extent a practical carpenter, and will be well supplied with all the usual tools of a carpenter. The following tools, however, are especially required by the carriage body-maker.

First, the workman will require a variety of draw knives, of different lengths and different bevels. For hard wood a short bevel is preferred, and for soft wood a long bevel. A medium bevel may be made to answer for both.

Second, a full set of framing chisels, one dozen in all, graded from a width of one-eighth of an inch to two inches wide. A dozen socket chisels for mortising will also be needed.

Third, several planes, with convex and concave surfaces, as well as perfectly straight planes.

Fourth, a variety of bits. You also want a hollow auger that can be set in a frame and used for cutting the tenons at the ends of spokes. There are hollow augers that are adjustable and will turn a tenon of the exact size required.

Fifth, a variety of rabbet knives, panel routers, rasps, and files.

Sixth, a good compass.

Seventh, hammers, screwdrivers, etc., etc.— the tools common to all carpenter shops.

The Wheel Bench. Of course, the carriage bodymaker must be provided with the ordinary carpenter's bench, with vises, etc. But in addition to that he must have a special wheel bench, which may be arranged with devices for driving spokes, boring tenons, driving on felloes, etc. The best bench would doubtless be the solid section of a tree, if one could be found as large in diameter as the largest wheel to be made, and if possible six inches larger, measuring from the centre out. A hole large enough to take the largest hub can be made in the centre, and at the bottom of this hole an upright bolt about an inch in diameter may be fixed securely, the upper end being provided with a square thread (or this bolt may be passed up from beneath). This serves as an axle. Blocks may be placed in the bottom of the hole to support the hub at the right height, and when the hub has been placed on the axle a plate with an inch hole in it may be laid over the top and screwed down by a thumb screw on the bolt. The opening in the hub for the box and axle should be filled at point and butt with solid blocks bored in the exact centre, the hole being just large enough to allow the upright bolt to pass. If this does not hold the hub firmly enough to allow of driving in spokes, a wedge may be placed at the side of the hub opposite the end of the spoke, so that the driving will come against the side of the solid block.

If such a trunk cannot be found, a bench may be made as follows: Get a hollow tree or log twenty inches in diameter, with a rim of two or three inches of solid wood under the bark. The log may be cut eighteen inches long, dressed, mortised like the hub of a wheel, (fourteen spokes are required), and heavy spokes driven in. A thick oak felloe is put on, and an iron tire two inches wide. On the upper sides of the spokes solid square oak pieces may be bolted, coming out to the rim of the wheel and extending to within a quarter of an inch of the hub. These should be made true and level, and plated on top with quarter inch iron. The wheel should be given a dish, the spokes rising upward, so that heavy pounding on the top may not make the wheel dish the other way, that is, the felloe sink below the level of the hub. This bench should be given several good coats of paint, and set up a firm base. The bolt with a thumb screw in the middle will be as in the preceding bench.

Attachments of the Bench. The bench should have a place especially arranged to give a grip below for a clamp to hold spokes down when being driven in. This might be, say, fifteen to eighteen inches from the hub. The clamp might be a simple affair, and a slit in the bench might allow it to be dropped down out of the way when not in use. If, now, a block of the proper height is placed under the spoke, and the spoke clamped lightly down upon it, it will be driven in at just the right angle.

At one side of the bench where it will not be in the way, there should be firmly fixed a sort of slide in which the frame of the hollow auger may be placed. A thumb screw below will permit of the frame being moved backward or forward, so that the auger may be brought up to the end of the spoke, whatever length it may be. At the same time, it should be arranged so that the auger may be taken out of the way when not in use, as it would interfere with setting the tire and similar operations.

Wheel Making. Much the most important

part of carriage building is the making of the wheels. More depends on the wheels than on any other single part, and to be of any value whatever they must be well made. At the same time, it is the wheel that most often needs repairing, and this cannot be done successfully except by some one who knows how to build a wheel.

The Material. The best wood for spokes, felloes, whiffletrees, neck-yokes, shafts, and similar parts is hickory. In case hickory is not available, ash may be used for spokes, and locust is even recommended. The hub should be of oak if the wheel is heavy, or elm if the wheel is light. In all cases the best wood, perfectly seasoned, is not only desirable, but almost absolutely necessary in wheel making. If the wood is not well seasoned it will shrink, and the moment it does the wheel comes to pieces. It is not quite so important that the hub be perfectly seasoned, as in shrinking it contracts and holds the spokes tighter; but the bands and similar irons are pretty sure to come loose in a short time if the hub is not well seasoned.

In these days spokes, hubs, and felloes are turned out in quantity at factories much cheaper than they can possibly be made, and much more neatly. Felloes may be bent or sawed,

the bent ones being preferred. Hubs should
not be mortised long before they are used, since
the sides of the mortise will dry out a little even
in the best seasoned wood, and shrink, causing
the sides of the mortise to concave, and so give
an imperfect surface for the spokes to adhere to.

Peculiarities of Wheels. The first thing to be
noted about a wheel is what is called its "dish."
If a wheel is so built that the spokes run at an
exact right angle to the centre of the hub,there
is danger that under strain they will work back
and forth, and under heavy strain of some kind
the wheel "dish" inward. The spokes should
turn outward from the hub very slightly,
the amount varying from a quarter of an inch
to three quarters, according to the size and character of the wheel. Wheelmakers have a variety
of ideas about the proper dish a wheel should
have; but the novice should in all cases follow
his pattern. If the dish is too great, it is obvious that with wear it will become greater. At
the same time there should be as little danger
as possible of the wheel being turned inside out,
so to speak, when it goes into a rut or runs
against a rock, or comes into collision with
another wagon.

A wheel must be set on the axle so that the
spokes will run perpendicularly down to the

ground (or very nearly so) and the tread of the tire will come flat and even on the ground. This of course throws all the dish of the wheel to the top, and at the top a pair of wheels is often two inches or more farther apart than at the bottom.

At the same time, the front wheels especially are given a slight "gather." The axle is so bent that the wheels have a tendency to come together. They are usually from a half to three quarters of an inch nearer together in front than behind. It is obvious that this makes the wheel wear toward the shoulder of axle, in spite of the taper of the axle spindle. When wheels are put on in this way, they do not necessarily come off if the nut works loose and drops off. The "gather" should be very slight, since it makes the wheels drag a little on the ground, and so run harder. A quarter of

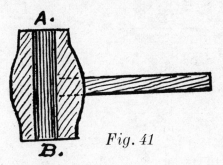

Fig. 41

an inch gather will not be noticed, however, and will often be of great value.

Hubs. Hubs should be bored very accurately through the centre, with a taper from the shoulder of the axle toward the nut, as shown in Fig. 41. The longer the spindle, the less the taper, of course. The hub is fitted inside with an iron "box," which is driven into the boring from the large end, and in this the spindle works. All hubs have an iron band fitted around the outer end, and most hubs have another around the end toward the axle. Large hubs liable to split have bands around the middle near the spokes, as shown by Fig. 42.

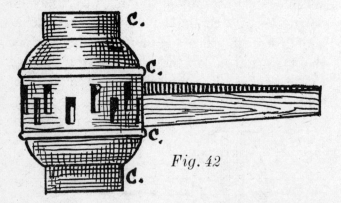

Fig. 42

In all light wheels the mortises are set in at perfectly straight row around the middle of the hub; but in very heavy hubs they are arranged as shown in Fig. 42.   This is called the "stagger" mortise.

It is extremely necessary that the mortises be cut very true, for a slight displacement of the mortise might throw the spoke an inch out of place.   A straight edge of sheet iron, form— a band about half an inch wide, may be put around the middle of the hub, and with the dividers it will be possible to see that the straight edge is all at points the same distance from the end of the hub,   Then a line may be drawn around the hub where the mortises are to be placed.   The exact outer circumference of the hub may be measured on this strip of sheet iron, and when this is laid out straight on the work bench it will be possible to divide it equally into twelve or fourteen parts, according to the number of spokes the wheel is to have. Then the places for the mortises may be accurately marked on the hub.

The spoke is slightly bevelled on the all four sides, and the mortise must have a corresponding inward bevel.   It will be observed in Fig. 41 that the spoke has a very decided bevel on the side toward the axle, or the inward side.   This has an important relation to the dish of the wheel.   Usually this bevelled side will be nearly perpendicular to the axis of the hub, and accordingly the spoke will be thrown slightly outward, to form the dish. The mortises should be cut a little smaller than the spokes, so that when the spokes are driven in they will not quite reach the iron box within the hub.

The Spokes. When the hub is ready, and the spokes are found to fit the mortises in the hub, the hub should be screwed firmly on the bench. Blocks with an inch hole in their centres for the bolt should be fitted into each end of the bore of the hub, and if necessary, the hub may be firmly supported by a block or wedge on the side opposite to which the spokes are to be driven. The mortises should be an inch or two above the level of the bench. A spoke may be put in its place, and six or eight inches from the outer end a block may be placed under it of just the right height to give the wheel the desired dish. Then the spoke may be held lightly on the block by means of the clamp already described.

It is a good idea to round off the corners of the tenons of the spokes with the hammer, and heat spoke ends and hub as much as possible without scorching, before dishing.

When all is ready for driving the spokes in, the insides of the mortises should be smeared with glue. Then the spokes may be driven in with sharp blows of a heavy mallet. A light hand hammer is not heavy enough. The wheel must now be left for the glue to dry, say a day or two, before further work.

For the next steps a bench such as that shown in Fig. 43 will be found useful.

First, the ends of the spokes must be sawed off at an even distance from the centre of the

Fig. 43

hub, about a sixteenth of an inch less than the diameter of the wheel is to be under the tire. The right length may be found by means of a simple gauge. A strip of wood a quarter of an inch thick and two inches wide may have an inch hole bored near one end, and this may be slipped over the bolt which serves as axle of the wheel on the bench. A smaller hole may be bored in which a pencil may be fixed at just the right distance from the central hole. With the gauge the workman may easily mark the ends of the spokes where he wishes to saw them off.

When they have been sawed off even, they should be tapered off to a blunt point, with the draw knife, thus preparing them for the boring of the hollow auger.

When the tenons have been bored so that the shoulder will just fit up against the inside of the felloe, the felloe pieces may be laid on the bench and marked for the holes to correspond to the tenons on the spokes. The diameter of these tenons and the corresponding holes in the felloe should be about a sixteenth less than half the width of the felloe.

The Felloes. Care should be taken to see that the felloes form a perfect circle. They are liable to get warped to one side or the other, and if they are out of gear it will be hard to get a true wheel.

The ends of the felloes where they come together to form the joints should be bevelled outward a little, so that the ends meet on the inside when in place (driven on the spokes), but do not quite meet on the outside. This will prevent the wheel from sagging at the joints. Also a sixteenth of an nich of extra wood should be allowed, so that if it is necessary to pass the saw between any two pieces to make the joints fit, the wheel will not be made too small.

The holes in the felloe should be small enough so that when the tenons of the spokes are driven into them, the felloe will stay in place securely without wedges; but in some cases it will be necessary to drive wedges lightly into the ends of the tenons. The end of the spoke should not come quite out to the outer edge of the rim, for if the spoke presses on the tire it is likely to cause the spoke to bend out of shape.

The joints of the felloes may be held securely by dowels, or wooden pegs passing through the ends which come together to form the joint, or by iron clamps fitting over the inside of the felloe. The latter are less likely to split the felloe, and in the hands of any but an expert workman are safer on that account.

When the felloe has been driven on, the gauge will be required to mark on the felloe the exact circumference of the circle which its outer edge should form.   When this mark has been made all around the wheel, the outer side of the rim may be planed off to the line with a concave plane.

Then the side of the felloe should be even up, and then by means of a suitable gauge, the outer side of the felloe should be made exactly perpendicular to the spokes.   One end of the gauge should touch the spokes at the hub, and the square should come true across the outer side of the felloe.   Owing to the dish of the wheel, and the subsequent plumbing of the spokes, this will make the edge not quite parallel with the central line of the hub, but when the wheel is on, the spokes will go straight down on a plumb line to the ground, and the tire will tread perfectly flat on the ground.

(It may be said that in practice, it is best that instead of having the spokes exactly plumb, they should turn in a little, say a quarter of an inch, on the ground, since under a heavy load the axles will spring a little, and that will bring the wheels to a true plumb.   It is under a heavy load that there is most need for the wheels to be exactly plumb.)

The wheels are now ready for the tires and

other irons, the putting on of which has already been described under "Carriage Ironing."

Repairing Wheels. If a wheel is dished a little too much when it is built, it will gradually become dished a great deal too much, the tire will become loose, and if not cared for the wheel will soon go to pieces. It is therefore an important matter to know how to take the dish out of a badly dished wheel.

Fig. 44

Fig. 44 shows the appearance of the end of the spokes of such a wheel. Not only is there a decided bevel on the side on which a bevel is expected, but the opposite side slants outward.

Fig. 45

Take off the tire of the wheel, carefully remove the rim in such a way as not to split it, and remove the spokes, working them back and forth till they come loose. Trim the upper side of the spoke as shown in Fig. 44, or the side that comes away from the wagon, perfectly straight, as shown in Fig. 45. Then carefully split the end and insert a wedge as close to the bevelled side as possible. This will throw the bevelled side out so as to fill up the mortise. Do not let the end of the wedge come against the box inside the hub.

In driving the spokes in again, if grease has accumulated in the mortises, wet the end of the spoke and dip in wood ashes.

If a wheel gets turned inside out by an accident, two or three strong men can usually pull it back so that it will dish the right way, and it can be tightened up by wedges in the mortises. Some of the wedges should be on the outside, though most should be on the inside. Those on the outside will prevent the wheel going to the opposite extreme and becoming too much dished.

In respoking old wheels, some have recommended boiling the hub in water containing saleratus, the saleratus to remove the grease. Boiling hubs is not to be recommended, since water is absorbed, the hub swells, and when it dries out again the spokes become loose and the irons come off. It is better to scrape out the mortises thoroughly with a knife, till the wood is well exposed.

If the mortises do not have to be recut, the spoke may simply be trimmed nicely so as to get the right angle, with very little dish, and the corners of the tenon that goes into the mortise rounded over by hammering. If this is not done the corners may prevent the sides of the tenon from taking a good grip on the wood of the hub.

Care should also be taken to see that the spoke will not touch the box of the hub when it is driven in. It is better to have it a little short.

Tires should always be reset as soon as they get loose. If the tire is allowed to run loose, sand will work in between it and the felloe and wear off the felloe till it becomes nearly ruined. Bent felloes can sometimes be straightened by soaking and bending them, allowing them to dry while held in position. They should be thoroughly dry before being put on.

It is a good plan to heat the ends of spokes before driving them in, as well as hubs, as much as can be done without scorching them. The spokes will then be held more tightly.

To remove boxes which stick, an old box that will fit inside may be heated red hot and dropped into the axle opening for a few minutes. This melts the grease and loosens the box, which may easily be driven out from the nut end.

If a box gets loose, some heavy manila paper may be cut in the form of a cross of Malta, the round centre being left just large enough to cover the end of the box, while some of the superfluous paper has been removed from the sides which hang down. Enough thicknesses of paper should be used to fill up the free space. Then the box is driven into place, and the large end is securely wedged. Of course the paper that may remain about the small end may be nicely trimmed away.

Something about Good Glue. Glue should not be allowed to stand more than twenty-four hours after it is mixed, or it will lose its power and decompose. The moment a bad odor is observed, a good workman will know that his glue-pot should be cleaned out and fresh glue prepared. The scum or skin that forms on the top of glue is worthless, and should in all cases be removed; and this must be done repeatedly. Only freshly melted glue has good adhesive properties.

Good glue is to be judged simply by its clearness. If glue as it comes from the factory is full of specks, it may be known that it is filled with foreign material, or has begun to decompose. It should be kept as nearly air-tight as possible, to prevent decomposition from **the** moisture in the air.

Use the glue very thin— the thinner the better. It should soak into the wood, and the faces of the wood come close together with no layer of glue between.

A Wheel for a Wheelbarrow. Making a wheel for a wheelbarrow is not difficult. Of course, the axle is fixed in the wheel, and runs in sockets on the barrow at each end. Three quarters of an inch is in most cases large enough. Any solid piece of wood, nicely rounded, may be used

Fig. 46

for the hub, which should be bound with an iron band on each side of the spokes. It will probably be best to arrange the mortises for the spokes in the stagger style (see Fig. 42), and

instead of being squared they may be **round.**
They should be bored as carefully and as evenly
as possible, one inch for wooden spokes, half an
inch (usually) for iron spokes. Iron spokes
will be most convenient, if the iron can be handled. Eight spokes will usually be sufficient.
A good arrangement is shown in Fig. 46. It
will be seen that the spokes are bevelled off at
the end where they come together inside the
hub. For iron hubs, half-inch iron rods will do
very well. A tenon is made on the rim end of
the spokes, which should set into a quarter or
three-eighths inch iron tire properly drilled.
The tenon ends should be a trifle smaller than
the spoke itself,— say three eighths of an inch,
if the spoke is iron and half an inch. If wooden
spokes are used, a felloe must be put on and
the wheel tired in the usual way. If iron spokes
are used, the spokes may run through the iron,
the tire being welded after the spokes are in
place and the tire set. The ends of the tenons
may then be filed off. Care should be taken
in rounding the tire, for any depression will make
the wheelbarrow run hard. If the rim is bent
over a model, the best results will be obtained.
Such a model may be made of wood and plated
with iron.

Making the Body of a Farm Wagon. It is

supposed in all cases of body making that the workman will have a pattern before him, either a complete wagon constructed nearly as he wishes, or something that will serve the purpose. It is not the aim of this book to go into wagon drafting, and it is not supposed that the user of this book will care to make landaus, victorias, etc. The following hints on making a farm wagon may prove useful.

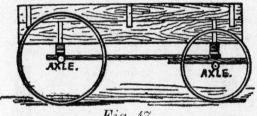

Fig. 47

Fig. 47 will show the side, woodwork only, of a modern farm wagon. The body should be eleven to twelve feet long, thirty-eight to forty-two inches wide, and seven eighths of an inch thick. The lower sides may be twelve to fourteen inches high, the upper sides six to nine inches. The upper boards should be good Norway pine, the cleats that hold them in place of ash. There is a toe-board at the top of the end piece of the lower sides, supported by iron braces. The end piece should be stiffened by cleats and fastened to the bottom by strap bolts.

The bolster in front (Fig. 48) should be a little over three inches wide and four and a half inches high in the middle. About twelve inches are allowed for the bearing surface. At the ends three inches will be high enough. The stakes taper up from three inches to an inch and a half at the top. They are mortised into the bolster with a tenon three quarters of an inch to an inch thick. The largest shoulder should be on the outside, say half an inch.

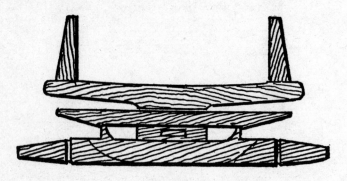

Fig. 48

The sandboard should be a little wider than the bolster, and, say, three inches deep. On each side of the reach it must be boxed a little for the hounds.

The hounds are cut out of two-inch stuff, cut to a pattern. Sometimes they are bent round at the back, sometimes united at the back by a sawed cross-piece, or they may even be attached to the reach. They are boxed out for the sand-board and axle so as to leave a clear space between the two of an inch and a half.

The axle beds are of hickory or maple—oak is sometimes used—and are four and a half by three or three and a quarter inches. Some form of steel or other thimble skein must be used, and the manufacturers of the skeins will give full details as to fitting the axle bed to the skein.

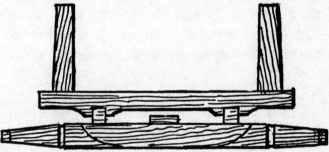

Fig. 49

The back bolster is about the same, or a little larger, than the front, and sets on the axle on the ends of the hounds on either side of the reach, as shown in Fig. 49.

There are two forms of pole used—the stiff
and the drop—and the hounds must correspond.
A good form of hounds, both back and front,
is shown in Fig. 50.   The back hounds lie above
the reach (or better, in the same plane with it).
The cross-bar of the front hounds lies on top of
the ends of the hounds, but runs under the
reach.   The ends which meet the pole are five
inches apart, and plated with iron, which re-
duces the opening to the size of the pole.   The
pole should be four inches square at the back,
tapering to two inches, and twelve feet long.
The back hounds are united by a plate of metal
where they meet the reach, and through this
plate a bolt passes.   The reach pole should
work freely, so that it may be pushed back or
drawn in, allowing adjusting the length of the
wagon.

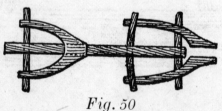

Fig. 50

The reach is two inches thick and four and a
half inches wide, and there should be half a
dozen holes which may be used for the bolt, in
varying the length of the wagon, the holes not

more than eight inches apart. The hounds should extend three feet forward of the back axle.

Prime white oak is best for most of the running gear, including bolsters, stakes, reach, etc. Black New York mountain birch is used for hubs in some cases, white ash or black oak for pole. All adjoining pieces should be put together with laps, leaving shoulders of one to three eighths of an inch. Glue is used to attach the cleats on the sides and endboards. When all the parts are shaped and ready, they should be dipped in warm raw linseed oil and put away for the oil to dry in. This makes a good foundation for paint, and preserves the wood where iron is joined on.

Ends of bolsters, etc., are bound with iron, but matters of this kind may be judged from the patterns followed.

Dimensions for wheels are as follows: Hubs, nine by ten and a half, outer end four and a half inches; spokes two and a half inches; pillars, one and three eighths; tread two and a half inches; wheels three feet eight inches and four feet six inches.

CHAPTER III.

CARRIAGE AND WAGON PAINTING.

In order to make a good job in painting a carriage or wagon, a place for doing the work is required which is free from all dust. A little dust will roll up under the brush and make no end of bad work. This is especially true when it comes to the varnish coats. In most buildings dust will accumulate on the rafters, and when the wind blows it will shake down a great deal of the dust. Before painting begins, such a room should be well dusted throughout several times, and a large canvas may be stretched over the wagon or carriage, care being taken to avoid canvas which will shed lint. Usually varnishing is done in a small, closely-ceiled varnish room, that may be heated, but a ventilator running up from the centre is desirable in order to secure a circulation of air for drying.

It is also very important that special care be used in removing all dirt, dust, or the like, which may get on the carriage in the natural order of the work. Carriages or wagons being repainted must be cleaned most thoroughly, even down into the smallest crevice or corner (also scraped with glass and sandpaper); and when pumice stone or the like is used, the corners must be well cleaned out with a dry brush, the ends of which have been moistened in varnish (but not enough to stick to the work). The little varnish will pick up the dust in corners where nothing else will. If the wagon is washed, it should be allowed to dry thoroughly before any attempt at painting is made, and then it should be dusted all over carefully with a proper duster. Just before each coat, also, the work should be most thoroughly dusted. It takes much longer to clean and dust than it does to lay on the paint or varnish.

Brushes. The first brush required is the round bristle brush, No. 0000 (four noughts). It is used for putting the priming on the body, etc. As the bristles are too long as they come from the store, they must be "bridled," or bound round with twine about half their length. A leather binding securely sewed is good. As the brush gets worn down the "bridle" may be removed and the brush is as good as ever.

A small round bristle brush or "sash tool" No. 8 is required to clean up around panels, between spokes, etc.

A flat camel's hair brush is best for laying

on color. Different widths will be required, according to the character of the work, from three-eighths to two inches. For laying color on small panels, or any very fine work, or for laying varnish, the flat or flowing badger hair brush is considered best, though camel's hair will answer every purpose.

For laying varnish on the body, or where it is desirable to have a brush that will carry a good deal of varnish, the oval chiseled brush, made of all white French bristles, is usually preferred. To accompany this, for cleaning up, a small flattened chisel brush is desirable.

Paints. A paint mill for grinding paints is almost a necessity.

For white lead in oil, only the very best can be considered even economical.

Raw linseed oil is the only oil used (boiled oil is not suitable).

Two kinds of varnishes are required, rubbing and finishing; the first for the coats that are to be rubbed, the latter for the final coat.

We also need brown japan and turpentine, and whatever colors may be desired. You will find it costs about half for paint if you mix your own colors, but it requires some skill to do it properly.

Always mix fresh paint for every job. Paint

that has stood exposed to the air becomes fatty, or oily, as the painters say. It sticks, and is unsuitable for carriage or wagon painting.

In mixing colors, always use a very little raw linseed oil to make the color elastic. If none is used the paint will crack and chip. A test may be made by putting a little on a piece of tin, and bending the tin when the paint is dry. The paint should bend with the tin, and not fly and crack in every direction. But the chief ingredients for mixing colors are usually japan and turpentine, about two tablespoonfuls of japan to a pint of the paint when mixed.

The paint should always be mixed in a perfectly clean dish, and if any skin appears, the paint should be strained through cheese cloth or muslin. Wire netting makes too coarse a sieve for carriage paint.

To mix colors, lay out the dry color on a proper stone and moisten with japan to a mush, mixing with a palette knife. Then add turpentine and grind through the mill with the mill screwed up as fine as possible. If too thin, the paint will not go through. When the paint is ground, add about a tablespoonful of raw oil to a pint of paint. Try the paint on the thumb nail, blowing it to hasten drying. It should have what is called an "egg-shell" gloss, not too bright or too dull. If it dries dull, add a trifle more oil; if too bright, add turpentine. The proportions of oil and turpentine vary with the color. Umber takes more oil, lampblack less, etc. Vermilion should be mixed with quick rubbing varnish, and no oil added, as oil darkens it. Glazing colors should also be mixed in varnish instead of oil and japan.

Great care should be used in selecting japan. Good japan does not curdle when mixed with raw linseed oil.

Prepared black should be thinned with turpentine to a cream-like consistency, and a very little raw oil added, until it dries with the egg-shell gloss. Too much oil is a detriment.

Putty is made by working whiting and dry lead into keg lead to a suitable consistency, and then adding a little brown japan to make the putty dry quickly.

Black putty for filling in around iron work which does not fit exactly, is made of three-fourths lamp black and one-fourth dry lead, mixed with japan. For putting in glass, equal parts of lamp-black and whiting mixed with equal parts of rubbing varnish and japan will be best. If the fibres of black velvet or plush are mixed with it, no rattling of a vehicle will jar the putty out. Usually putty should be colored to the color of the job. Common putty, like common paint, should never be used on a wagon.

One Method of Carriage Painting. As soon as the woodwork is ready, before the irons are put on, cover the wood with a coat of priming made of oil and a little white lead, with a small amount of japan if it is desired that the job dry in a hurry. The oil is the main thing, and soaks into the wood, including all parts to be covered with the irons, and the lead fills up some of the pores. When it has stood two days or thereabouts, sandpaper with No. 2 paper, and fill up the largest nailholes with white putty, or putty made according to the first recipe, and colored.

Next put on the body (but not on the gears) the first coat of lead. A suitable amount of keg lead, say two pounds, is worked soft with oil, and an equal amount of japan added. This is thinned to the proper consistency with turpentine. A rather light coat that will cover the ground is all that is needed. It is well when this coat is dry to go over all hardwood parts and fill the seams with a putty made of equal parts of dry lead and whiting, mixed with equal parts of japan and rubbing varnish. This will dry in a couple of hours, and the whole may be sandpapered with the paper used on the priming coat. All that is necessary is to smooth the paint, not to scour it all off.

For fine work we now follow with from two to five coats of "rough stuff." Fireproof paint, Ohio paint, Grafton paint, and English filling are one and the same, though English filling costs much more than the others. Mix either of these with an equal weight of keg lead, and add equal parts of brown japan and rubbing varnish. When run through the mill loosely it should be thinned to good working consistency with turpentine. Dust the job carefully and apply one coat after the other without sandpapering. Apply only to the larger panels.

The wagon now receives the irons, the gears having had only the priming.

If the gears are to be vermilion or any other bright color, the first lead coat (put on after ironing) should be slightly colored with the same color. This lead coat consists of keg lead mixed with enough oil to permit its being worked up. Half as much japan as oil is added, and the whole run through the mill, when the paint is thin with turpentine so that it will spread easily. Care should be taken to cover the gears below as well as on top, and finish up all bolts, nuts, etc,. perfectly.

While the gear is drying, we may proceed to

rub out the rough stuff on the panels. For this purpose we need pumice stone (cut across the grain with an old saw), a pail of water, sponge and chamois skin. Light, open-grained pumice is the best. Its grain may be seen if it is dipped in water. When the pumice lump has been sawed through so as to give an even surface, it is smoothed by being rubbed on a smooth stone. The panel is rubbed in a circular movement, or lengthwise of the panel, not too hard so as to tear the paint, and with plenty of water to keep the heat down. A very light dark coat is sometimes put on top of the rough stuff. When this is all rubbed off even it is supposed that the surface is smooth. It is now well washed, corners, etc., being washed out with a small brush or "water tool," and all dried with chamois.

Next let us putty up the gears with equal bulk of keg lead and whiting beaten together with a mallet and thinned a trifle with japan. All holes and imperfections should be carefully filled. In an hour or two rub down the putty with used sandpaper and carefully dust off.

The upper and exposed parts of the gear may now be covered with paint made of keg lead mixed soft with turpentine, with a gill of japan to a pint of paint, and, if time for drying can be allowed, a tablespoonful of raw oil. The whole should be colored as before, and the paint laid on smoothly and evenly.

We are now ready to paint the body. The whole should be sandpapered with the finest sandpaper. Sometimes a body color is laid on; but in most cases the final color may be laid directly on the rough stuff. The color is mixed with turpentine, and about two tablespoonfuls of japan to a pint, with one tablespoonful of raw oil.

A coat of color may be laid on the gears in the same way. A second coat of color will follow in a few hours, on both gear and body.

We now rub the surface of the paint with moss or curled hair, and apply a coat of rubbing varnish mixed with the color. This coat should not be slapped on, though it is to be rubbed down.

The gears should be rubbed well before putting on the first coat of color. Usually one coat is sufficient, and when it has dried two or three hours we may put on a heavy coat of rubbing varnish mixed with a little color.

Allow the varnish coats two days to dry.

When the varnish coat is dry, it should be rubbed with pulverized pumice, on the body, while rubbing with curled hair will do for the gears.

To rub the body nicely, begin at the top and work down. No. 12 or No. 14 pulverized pumice is required, with woolen rags, water, sponge, and chamois. Double the rag up, wet it, and dip it in the pumice, and begin rubbing, bearing on rather hard. You can tell by the touch when the surface has been made sufficiently smooth. When you have rubbed sufficiently, wash well, and rub dry with the chamois. As before, a small brush will be needed to get the stone all out of corners, etc.

The gears are rubbed in the same way with curled hair or moss.

Body and gears are now ready for striping. The painting is complete, and varnishing alone remains.

The Putty Method of Painting. A cheaper method of painting is by what is called the "putty" process, which takes the place of rough stuffing.

Apply the priming and the first coat of lead as already described. Then mix keg lead with turpentine and japan to the consistency of a stiff paste, adding a little of the color the vehicle is to be painted. Put this onto a small portion of the body (three or four panels) with a stiff brush, and then, when the turpentine has evaporated and the color is quite dead, work it into all the pores of the wood with a broad-bladed putty knife. Then scrape off clean all that has not been taken up by the pores. When the whole job has been covered, it may be set aside to dry.

The gears may be treated in the same manner. A piece of stout leather will serve for rubbing the putty coat into the spokes, etc.

When dry, sandpaper down nicely and apply the color at once.

The Wood Filler Method. The wood filler takes the place of the priming. It is put on the framework before the panels are put in, and then on the panels. Then the usual rough stuff is put on, mixing it as follows: 3 parts Grafton paint, 2 parts keg lead, 2 parts oil japan, 1 part rubbing varnish. This is also put on the panels before they are fitted. It makes a nicer job around the fitting, and requires less labor.

After the filling, the gears are ironed, and all rubbed down with No. 3 sandpaper. We then put on a lead coat of keg lead, oil, japan, and turpentine, and putty up all openings. Two coats of lead with color in it should follow, and then the color coat and color varnish, ready to be mossed off.

Varnishing. To get a good varnish finish, a uniform degree of heat should be maintained, which requires a heating apparatus in the varnish room. A self-feeding coal stove may be set up near the partition outside of the varnish room, the partition at that place being sheet iron. All the rubbing with water, etc., should be done in the paint room, for no dust and no water should ever be allowed on the floor of the varnish room.

The striping and lettering is done over the first and only color varnish coat. Then comes a coat of clear rubbing varnish, which must be rubbed in the paint room with pulverized pumice and water, as before described. When the body has been returned to the varnish room, it should be dusted, the ends of the duster being dipped lightly in a little varnish held in the hand and then rubbed off so it will not stick.

For ordinary work the flat bristle brush is best.

In rubbing varnish, great care must be taken that the pumice has no sand or grit in it; the pail, water, rub-rags, chamois, etc., must be perfectly clean, and of course the hands of the varnishers must be thoroughly washed,— and not in the pail, either. The pumice should not be allowed to dry on the surface, but should be washed off frequently till the surface is quite clean.

As the varnisher lays on the varnish, he first passes the wet sponge lightly over the work to take off any remaining dust, and then does the rough portions of a panel or the like first.

In rubbing, corners, angles, etc., need not be touched, as there is danger of cutting through the paint, and nothing is gained.

Put on plenty of varnish, and pick out any specks that may appear, with sharpened whale-bone.

The first coat should stand at least two days, and if possible four days, before being rubbed. The rubbing is directed chiefly to getting out all specks, etc. If the job is not a particular one, curled hair rubbing will do. A second coat of rubbing varnish is now added.

The third coat (of finish varnish) will be the finishing coat. When it has been laid on nicely the job is done.

Ornamenting. As we have already stated, the ornamenting goes over the color varnish coat.

For striping, small round brushes, known as striping pencils, are used. These are commonly of camel's hair, though ox-hair brushes are good for rough wagon striping. They range in size from one-eighth inch up, and should be at least two and a quarter inches long. If shorter, it will be hard to make the stripe straight.

Striping is an art that must be learned, and little can be said here which will help the amateur. The pencil is held between the thumb and forefinger, the other fingers being used to steady the hand. The main thing is a good eye, and plenty of practice.

A zinc palette is probably the best, as it can easily be kept clean. It may be cut from any smooth piece of zinc.

Small tin cups will do to hold the color.

After use, the pencils should be well cleaned in turpentine, and they should be kept in a dusttight box with a piece of glass at the bottom on which to spread the pencils. It is a good idea to grease them with sweet oil after cleaning.

Colors for striping may be mixed the same as body colors. Tube colors are not recommended, as they are too "short"—do not flow readily from the brush.

Ornamental striping, or fancy striping requiring turns, etc., must be done with a short brush, say half an inch long.

Nowadays it is hardly worth while to attempt any lettering or ornamenting other than striping, since it is posssible to purchase transfers or decalcomania with all kinds of lettering, pictures, etc., most perfectly executed and easily varnished on; or patterns, stencils, etc., may be used with far better results than can be secured by handwork.

A homemade transfer may be made as follows: Paint the design on the gummed side of a sheet of gummed paper, like that used for postage stamps. When dry, press down upon this another gummed sheet that has been evenly moistened and let it dry between the leaves of a book. When dry, dampen the back of the sheet on which the drawing was made, and when soft enough remove it. The design is transferred to the panel by transfer varnish or rubbing varnish, and when dry, the paper dampened and removed as before. This is much easier than trying to do the work on the panel, and you can experiment till you get a good drawing.

THE END.

Date Due

FEB 4 1986		
FEB 2 7 1989		
SEP 2 6		
MAY 0 8 1999		
MAR 1 1 2003		